Dimly Lit

Emily Zondlak

Chapbook Press

Schuler Books
2660 28th Street SE
Grand Rapids, MI 49512
(616) 942-7330
www.schulerbooks.com

Dimly Lit

Paperback ISBN 13: 9781948237116

Library of Congress Control Number: 2018959687

eBook ISBN: 9781948237154

Photography by Ariel Huffman

Copyright © 2018 Emily Zondlak
All rights reserved.

No part of this book may be reproduced in any form without express permission of the copyright holder.

Printed in the United States by Chapbook Press.

A thank you to Ariel Huffman from Love Anchors
Photography for capturing awesome images!

Backstory

A little backstory is that I wrote this book when I was immature and didn't have a relationship with my Lord Jesus Christ. Hence this is the reason behind the title, Dimly Lit. God has totally changed my life and outlook on life ever since I chose to follow Him as my Lord and Savior in October of 2009!

I just wanted to share this with you before you embark upon your reading journey!

Table of Contents

How It All Began
Life on County Road 36
The Apple Orchard
Forest Grove Elementary
Houses in the Woods
Races of a Lifetime
Swing Village
Liar, Liar pants on Fire
Vacation, All I Ever Wanted!
Changing of the Aides
5th Grade Getaway
A Dream Come True
We Thought They'd Never End
First Boyfriend
School's Out for Summer
Tragic Senior Year
My College Experience

Preface

Imagine your doctors telling you that your four-month-old daughter has a disability called Cerebral Palsy. The doctors can tell this by the baby smiling more than a "normal" baby her age. How would you react to this situation? Maybe you would feel you and your spouse's world flip upside down. Would you keep your disabled daughter or would you give her up for adoption? Doctors have begun your daughter with therapy. You and your spouse are doing everything that the doctors are telling you to do. Some days you may feel like you are doing the wrong thing.

While the months flow by, you, your spouse, and maybe your other children are living life as normal as possible with your Cerebral Palsy (CP) daughter, You may start to receive special equipment for your daughter to help with standing, sitting, bathroom needs, feeding needs, walking, etc. When your daughter reaches the age of two or three years old, she may receive her first manual wheelchair because of her disability.

Specialists say that your daughter is ready to start school when she may be three years old, but you and your spouse are not ready for that. You start the process of getting your CP daughter ready for that big milestone. A lift bus arrives in your driveway and you watch or help the bus driver buckle your daughter up. You hug and say your good-byes to your daughter while tearing up. While crying, the bus driver escorts you off the bus and tells you that everything and your daughter will be fine.

While watching the bus drive away what seems like slow motion, the Bible verse Jeremiah 29:11 pops in your head. "For I know the plans I have for you," declares the LORD, "plans to prosper you and not to harm you, plans to give you hope and a future." You are ready to see what your daughter's life will be about. You and your family will experience your CP daughter's life experiences.

How It All Began

My parents were high school sweethearts. My dad ran track after school and my mom would make up an excuse so that my dad would have to drive her home if she did not have cheer practice. They dated for eight years, and of course, they broke up a couple of times in the eight years. My mom wrote him a bunch of love letters and my dad kept every one. She said that she was crazy in love back then, but I think she is still kind of crazy in another way.

My dad has black and white short hair parted on the side. My mom's hair is short brown with white in it. She spikes it and it stands out in every direction. My dad has brown eyes and so do I. My dad loves to start trouble by playing jokes and saying smart remarks in a cocky way. My mom isn't as fun or joking as he is, but she can be fun in her own way. She is much more serious than my dad who is a goof ball. I guess you can say that I am a good mix between the two. I love to goof around, but I can be serious if I need to be. I am the youngest child of three girls in my family. I have older twin sisters named Britney and Ashley. They are fraternal twins, so they look similar, but are very different in both personality and style. They are two years older than me, so it is very nice to be the younger sibling and be protected and pampered by both of them.

    I wanted to remember fond memories of growing up. I thought the best way was to start writing down my life as I remembered it. Also I wanted to share my life before I surrendered my life to Jesus Christ and did not have passion for Him. I take rabbit trails throughout my book to give insight on Biblical truths.

Life on County Road 36

     Where I lived during my first few years of my childhood was in a ranch style home where I had my own room with little heart wallpaper. My curtains were red and my blinds perfectly matched. As I became older, my changing table became my toy and stuffed animal holder. I also remember having a pink and white toy box stuffed with toys. When I was six years old, I received my big girl bed. It was just two mattresses assembled together with red sheets and a baby rail, so that I wouldn't fall out, but it was great to feel so big that a crib was no longer required. I had a big tall blue dresser with white knobs next to my bed. My closet stored not only my clothes, but I remember it being filled with medical equipment, pull-ups, and cases and cases of Pediasure. I was not getting enough nutrients at the time, so Pediasure became a staple in my diet. I did not mind because I loved the taste of it.

The living room was a big long room, which was split up by having the dining room table by the slider door and all of the furniture on the other side by the window. My sisters, Britney, Ashley, and I would play video games non-stop. I remember some of the games we played were called: Zaga, Pac-Man, Power Rangers and the crazy little blue haired dude, Sonic. Also we played on our swing set with our neighbors or by ourselves when the weather was nice. My parents and sisters would put me in my swing and push me, give underdogs, and make me spin in circles. I would laugh when they did those things because it would sometimes make my body feel weird. Under our swing-set, there was golden sand and my sisters would dig huge holes until they got to the black sand. Of course, I would dig too until I reached to the black sand also, because I wanted to be just like them. I did not like the feeling that I had sand in my teeth. I still cringe when thinking about it. Sometimes we would jump on the neighbor's tramp and I would get tossed up really high. It was fun for me because all I had to do is sit there, and they would do all the hard work of jumping up and down to make me go up high. One-time our parents bought us a blow up pool and the neighbors came to swim. It was "the cool thing" for a while. Then we had a slip-n-slide and my sisters and I loved that. The only thing I didn't like about it was the grass sticking to me. We also had a Barbie car, which my sisters would let me ride while they drove. I think that I drove it once in a while, if they were feeling generous. I remember many fun times with my sisters and sometimes wondered whom I would have played with if I were an only child?

Just before our property line ended my dad built a fire pit and my family would have fires at night, and of course, we would make delicious s'mores. When it was the first day of summer, we would have one just to kick off the summer. I loved having fires back then because it was our family time being all together. My sisters and I would sometimes play with sticks in the fire, but always being very careful. Our elderly neighbors had a huge tree on their property, so my sisters would climb it while I played and watched them from the bottom of the tree. I would always smile and laugh because once they got to the top, it seemed as though they just would daydream and take in the country air.

The Apple Orchard

Pondering back to my earliest childhood memory, I was only three years old, but I can recall riding on the lift bus on the way to preschool. I sometimes had my Winnie the Pooh backpack on my tray of my wheelchair, and I would play with it on my way to school. I can still remember the corner that the lift bus turned down, heading toward my school. Every time I came to that corner, I would say to my parents, "Go that way." as I pointed toward my preschool, as if every destination outside my home would be my preschool. My school was named Apple Orchard and it had three different rooms that the students played in. Each room had different toys to play with, and in one room it had a tree house where we, the students, could read books. I only got to sit in the tree house one-time because you had to climb stairs to get up to it and I wasn't able to accomplish that on my own because of my disability. Once in a while we would go to a huge gym to play, listen to music, and watch movies on a big screen, which seemed like paradise for kids at the time. My speech teacher was an old man who was bald. When I had speech class with him, it felt like an eternity because of his dry personality. During the school day, I required an aide for assistance because of me being in a wheelchair. I do not recall many details of my first aide, just that not every student in school had one.

As I remember, I had an aide who was really heavy set. I want to say her name started with a "M" for some reason. She was the aide that pushed my wheelchair to speech class. After school, she also waited with me for the bus to come, but that was the extent of her duties and my time with her during the day. When the school day was done, I waited for the bus with a girl who was my age. She also was in a wheelchair. I remember she had long blonde, almost white hair. Our wheelchairs were set perfectly side-by-side to each other, as if we were at the starting line of a race of some sort.

Sometimes, I had a hand-sized baby that I loved to play with. It would always keep me company until the lift bus arrived.

After school, I would watch my favorite TV shows that were, *Gulla Gulla Island, Blue's Clues,* and *Timmy the Tooth*. Sometimes I held my Timmy the Tooth stuffed animal while I watched the *Timmy the Tooth* show. Some days I wondered why my sisters had school and I didn't. I did not realize back then that I did not have to attend preschool everyday of the week. All I knew was that I had the house and my mom to myself, and that I could watch my favorite TV shows all day, as if I were on a vacation. I sat in my high chair and ate while watching each cartoon episode, mesmerized, even if I had seen it dozens of times before. I attended Apple Orchard for two years during preschool. This is where it all began, my obstacles, the outsider feeling, and schools I as look back. I could not even imagine anything bigger than this, but then I started kindergarten at Forest Grove Elementary.

Forest Grove Elementary

At Forest Grove, I was the first handicapped person to be put in that school. I had an aide named Mrs. Vroogd, but I called her Mrs. O because I liked the two o's side-by-side in her name. Besides, saying her name was too hard for me to say. So that is how she got her name, Mrs. O. In kindergarten, the janitor made a tar path just for me on the playground, so that I could go outside with my wheelchair during recess. I met my best friend Laura, and we were inseparable. We hung out all day at school. We played at her house and in February, Laura was in the hospital for a while. My mom and I gave her a rose one-day when we went to see how she was doing. Laura and I played in the playroom, while our moms talked. When my mom and I left, Laura gave me a little purple bear so that I would not be lonely at school without her. Rachel became my best friend while Laura was in the hospital. When Laura came back to school, that's when the fights began. The competitions and quarrels lasted the rest of the school year. I thought I could not have two best friends back then. I had two sisters, why couldn't I have two best friends? One-day at recess, all three of us had it out. Rachel and Laura put me in the middle and made me choose which one of them I wanted to be my best friend. What a dilemma at such a young age! I cannot believe how many times I went back and forth between them. Thank goodness Annie showed up, and Laura became her best friend. Rachel then decided to become Sara's best friend. So in the end of my kindergarten year, I was without a best friend after all the disputes. I still had Mrs. O, who was my adult best friend though. (I hope that you don't mind rabbit trails on what I learned by studying the Word of God. Prepare for more rabbit trails!) And of course, I didn't know how to love or handle arguments as Jesus teaches in His Word.

In first grade, I had a crazy teacher named Mrs. Ski, who was fun and upbeat. I remember she said that we, the students, would always sing this chant when we would write this certain word and will never forget it. To this day, she is right. The word is vacation and the chant goes like this: V-A-C-A-T-I-O-N. We're gonna have a ball. VACATION!

I remember reading this certain bunny book and I looked at the pictures a lot more than I actually read the book. It was about a little kid bunny that was scared to go to the doctor for a checkup. So he asked questions of his friends, the turtle, frog, and owl. The day before his appointment, his mom planned to talk to her son about his fear. I remember that she did not have to because his friends helped him with it. I had a favorite page in that book and it was where the author showed the bunny's body in an X-Ray machine. For some reason, I would lick that page where the little bunny would have the X-Ray machine on him because I loved that page. I know, it sounds weird, but that is what I did back then. On the bus I would lick the page just a few times, but when I was alone I licked it a lot more. Maybe back then I knew that it was dumb of me to be licking it so I only licked it a lot when I was alone. This must have been my way to express that I really liked something, and it seemed to be the only logical thing to do.

Holiday parties were the best at Forest Grove. Each teacher had a project with something that the students could make and that was fun to do. At the Halloween party in first grade, we played a game where the students could not move for a long time. I was on my stomach with my head facing the floor. I was dressed in a bunny costume, and I stayed in the game for the longest time.

On Valentine's Day, Mrs. O gave me a small bear magnet. It was white with a pink hair ribbon on its ear and it was holding a hot pink heart that had the words "Be Mine" on it. When you squeezed the heart, it played a song, but you had to squeeze really hard for it to play. I carried that around for a couple weeks then I stuck it in my special box.

    Mrs. O gave me a small stuffed bunny for Easter. It was white with purple floppy ears. It had a light pink nose and a little bit of white spiky hair in between its floppy ears. It had a round, white tail. I took that bunny everywhere I went and my mom would have to wash it at night while I was sleeping because I would get that poor bunny dirty.

Houses in the Woods

My family and I were living in an apartment while our new house was being built. My parents decided to build because the house would fit my accessibility needs, such as, wider doorframes, ramps, spacious bathrooms, and hardwood floors. Back to my memories at the apartment of the woods! My sisters took turns sharing a room with me because it was a three-bedroom apartment, and there were the five of us. Ashley shared a room with me first. She would tell jokes at night and I would try to laugh quietly so our parents would not hear us or else we would get in trouble. Ashley would say this fake prayer and I would laugh. It went like this: Now I lay me down to sleep, a bag of peanuts at my feet. If I shall die before I wake, I shall die with a tummy ache. (Rabbit trail. At this age, I did not understand the importance or the effectiveness prayers have on a person's life.)

Our beds were diagonal from one another, my pink and white toy box was below one of the windows, and there was a little white dresser below the other window. I remember Ashley and Britney shared a little white desk next to the dresser that for some reason, I am picturing a total mess with papers on it going every direction. Ashley and I shared the closet and all I remember is that it had big doors. One-time Ashley watched an episode of *Scooby-Doo* and she had nightmares and was talking in her sleep. I do not think either of us received very much sleep that night. At the foot of my bed, I had my toy cash register. At that point of my life, I thought that the toy cash register was so neat. It was red with yellow keys and a blue drawer, and I cherished it as if it had real money in it. (Rabbit trail. A cherished object is not what Jesus Christ wants; for He is a jealous God. Christ wants a wholehearted devotion and an intimate relationship. I hope that you don't mind rabbit trails on what I learned by studying the Word of God.)

The little dining room was where my family spent most of the time, and usually, it resulted in weird family conversations. The room was shaped like a circle with little square windows at the very top. It seemed like back then, even the simplest of things were entertaining to my sisters and I. One night at dinner, my mom thought that I was looking out of the corner of my eyes. So she tested me and I was not. Another time my sisters and I were eating oatmeal for breakfast. We thought it was funny to have the oatmeal on one side of the bowl so the other side was bare. (Rabbit trail. Christ wants His children to have simple faith, obedience, and trusting Him in everything.)

The living room was long and big. I saw trees and leaves from the patio slider. The fall weather reminds me of the song ""Blink"" by Revive. The meaning behind this song is: don't take life for granted. Slow down and enjoy life.

Looking back, it seemed like a very small apartment for our entire family, but it was adventurous and seemed like a fun camping trip.

Races of a Lifetime

The very first time I won a medal was when I ran a Memorial Day race when I was in the first grade. I was so proud of myself. In the third grade, the gym teacher set up a mini-race track just for me because my age group ran around on the grass. It was hard for me to run on the grass because of my wheelchair. I had to wheel around my track twice, just to make it fair for the other students. My dad helped direct me around the course. I went to the finish line as the other students were heading there too. I felt like everything was in slow motion, but I was the first girl in my class to give a high-five to a teacher. I received a medal. I was so enthusiastic about my medal, but I only wore it for half the day.

In the fourth grade, I ran the big race with my dad. We ran the entire path as fast as we could, but this race was not as successful as my previous grades races. We were the second to last ones to finish the race. As the saying goes, you can't always finish first! (Rabbit trail. Your actions are a billboard. What are your actions saying? Are you living for Jesus Christ daily or running away from Him? What you do, springs from your heart.)

Swing Village

In second grade, Mrs. O left me to go to Florida without a sub for what seemed like two weeks. So Mrs. Unicorn was my sub aide in her place. She was also the second grade teacher, so she was doing two jobs at once. I remember my huge table was a mess because she didn't put anything away. I couldn't handle the mess. I was glad to go to Mrs. Bubbly's (my Resource teacher's) room for the afternoon because I didn't like my messy table. Mrs. O always put everything back in its place.

Everybody in my class was on the TV news. The reporters said to us, "You can wave and say, 'Hi Mom and Dad' or just smile.'" I just smiled. The people who said, "Hi Mom and Dad" you couldn't hear it on the news. So it looked funny. I was glad I chose just to smile at the camera.

I can remember in second grade, Rebecca wanted to sit next to me while I was in my foam chair during reading time. I didn't like her because she acted like a mom toward me. So I wasn't good friends with her because she annoyed me and was one of those "fake" friends. You know, one of those people who are nice and caring one day, and the next day, they ignore you.

On a field trip, our class went to this place called Swing Village. I can remember seeing two mannequins, wearing big wooden shoes when we pulled up. Outside in the warm morning sunshine, we saw a large fake stork holding onto a cloth in its beak where the baby would be. There was not a baby bird in the cloth, so Mrs. O put me in the cloth and took my picture with two friends standing behind me. Then I saw the high swing ride where you are sitting in a chair and the ride swings you around in circles. I wanted to go on it, but the dilemma was the ride called for one person to a swing. Mrs. O talked to the person who was running the ride into letting her and I ride in a swing together. I laughed so much on the ride.

(Rabbit trail. There are situations in life when you don't want to go through them. You may feel like turning around and running away from the tough situation. When the world seems to be a wrack, turn to Jesus because He has everything planned!)

Liar, Liar pants on Fire

In third grade I lied frequently, so I got in trouble and yelled at a lot by Mrs. Lips. Mrs. Lips was a tall, young, and a newly married lady, who didn't like us, kids to misbehave. For some reason, she found out that I was lying to her. She talked to Mrs. O behind my back one day and I saw them talking outside of the door of the classroom. I was throwing a paper towel away and I looked in the hall for no reason. There they were standing, Mrs. Lips talking sternly to Mrs. O about me lying. The look on Mrs. O's face was a look that I never had seen before. I went back playing with a water baby that cried real tears if you fed it its bottle.

One time, Mrs. Lips wrote in my notebook to my mom about what I had done that was bad. While Mrs. Lips was writing the letter, I was on the verge of crying, but I bit my lip to avoid crying. When she allowed me to leave, I cried in the hall by the gym so that nobody would hear me. Mrs.

Dimly Lit

Bubbly, my Resource teacher, also got after me about lying. That is why I am so honest today, because of my experiences in the third grade with Mrs. Lips and Mrs. Bubbly yelling at me. I felt so awful and I did not want them to be disappointed with me, so I stopped lying in school. Sometimes people who are close to me, joke around with me and say in a teasing tone, "You know Em, it is OK to lie some times." I just smile and laugh.

(Rabbit trail. Often people are caught up in the moment of things. Actions or words can complete one of two things. They can help others or knock someone down. Too often words drag people down. Words are powerful so use them wisely. Love makes all the difference in life when it's Christ's love. Being there for others, listening to them, giving hugs or smiles can make people's days. Be bold and courageous because blessings may flow your way. Pray constantly because God wants to help you every step of the way!)

Vacation, All I Ever Wanted!

My family's Disney cruise trip was awesome! We were on land for three days and on the cruise ship for four days. My dad had our whole trip planned out just because he is a-planner-kind-of-man. I remember the cruise ship because my sisters and I loved being on such a fabulous boat. I can only remember some things that we did as a family on land, mainly when we went to Disneyworld. I recall my first experience on a roller coaster while we were there. Space Mountain is the ride I really got scared on because the ride is in the dark and you are all over the place. Upside down, quick turns, and you are not buckled in. To this day, I will not go on that ride and my family still kind of teases me about it. (Rabbit trail. Fear is a feeling that many people allow it to control their lives. Jesus Christ is with you! You can control your emotions instead of letting them control you. Pray through your fear and when you have accomplished/overcame your fear, you'll be satisfied!)

My family and I were eating breakfast outside one morning sitting at a table with an umbrella while on vacation in Disney. The sun was out, but it was not that hot out yet and so we were relaxing and taking our time. There was an elderly couple eating a few tables down from us and they finished eating before us. I was acting like my normal self, laughing and happy. When they were finished eating, the elderly man gave me a small miniature Winnie the Pooh bear because he was amazed how I interacted with my family. I think it was because I am disabled, was in my wheelchair, and had not acted as though I was handicapped.

On another family vacation, we went to Cedar Point in Ohio. My dad had to ride all the rides with me because my mom would say she would hold all of our things, but I knew the truth. I knew she was scared of the rides.

In the winter months starting in January, my family and I skied every Sunday all afternoon. My mom did not ski because she was afraid of falling and getting hurt. So she stayed in the lodge and ate junk food while she watched us ski. I skied on four skis, belted in a seat with my dad tethering behind me. I steered down the hill by shifting my weight from side-to-side. Sometimes we skied really fast because it was fun going that speed. That lasted for 12 weeks. At the end of the season, the group had a huge dinner for all of the skiers and helpers. The skiers received little gold medals. I skied for two years with that group. At the second dinner, the skiers received a different gold medal. It was cool to receive a medal; it felt as though it was the winter Olympics.

Changing of the Aides

School year had started and I was in the fifth grade (the top dog in the school, finally) and things started moving fast when I met Mrs. Van, my soon-to-be new aide.

Every Thursday afternoon, Mrs. O had to go her class at University so Mrs. Van, a new aide, was with me during that time. In November and December, Mrs. Van came a couple times in the morning because she wanted to see what the morning routine was like. By then, Mrs. Van was comfortable with the afternoon routine, so I did not think anything of her being there in the morning in addition to Mrs. O.

One day at lunchtime, a lunch lady told me that Mrs. O was leaving and was not going to be my aide anymore. I didn't think or react back then, as I would have now because of my age. So in the summer, I wrote a letter to Mrs. O thanking her for everything that she bought me and I wrote lyrics to songs that reminded me of her. Looking back, I wish that I wrote about memories that we had together, but at that age, I didn't know I would want to reflect on it and what an impact that Mrs. O would have on me. I hid my letter underneath my dresser until the day before Mrs. O's final day with me.

    The D-day of Mrs. O leaving had arrived. That day all that I wanted to do was be by her side, but I could not bring myself to do it because I was so sad. Also I wanted to hug her all day. I felt my heart was overflowing with love for her. We exchanged our gifts in the morning and I gave her a real diamond necklace. She gave me a jewelry box that plays a song. When the afternoon came, I went to Mrs. Bubbly's room and waited until Mrs. O's surprise party started in the fifth grade classroom. I let her go in first. My family was there and Mrs. O gave her speech to our class. Then she opened her gifts and everyone had cake, but I did not want any.

The clock struck 3:30 P.M. and everyone left the classroom to go home so it was just Mrs. O and I in the classroom alone. She took me out of my wheelchair and we hugged for a long time (like a bear hug). I noticed that she was crying when she took me out of my wheelchair and while we were hugging, my heart sunk from that moment on. I honestly did not think I would get through this farewell, which was a celebration for everyone, but Mrs. O and I. My family helped her husband and son pack up Mrs. O's van. My family showed their gratitude and said their good-byes to Mrs. O.

I rode the bus home because I wanted to be alone for a couple minutes so that I could think without interruption. On the bus, I had to wait for my bus driver because she was saying good-bye to Mrs. O. My lunch hour aide named Mrs. Eccentric, knocked on the window, waved with a big smile and wrote my name on the window. I smiled, laughed, and waved back. Next, my replacement aide, Mrs. Van, came on the bus and said, "I want to see a happy Emily when we come back after Christmas break!" I just smiled and thought: *Yeah right! Whatever!* as she walked off the bus.

After Christmas break, I was not excited to return to school and have my new aide, Mrs. Vanduel Hug. My first impression of her was not very promising. I met her for the first time before Christmas break, after my lunch hour in Mrs. Bubbly's room. Mrs. Van shook my hand and said, "Hi! My name is Mrs. Vanduel Hug, but you can call me. . . Mrs. Van." in a high squeaky voice. She was acting "fake" like people do around me when they see me because I am disabled. I thought: *Oh great! You are one of "those" people. This is going to be fun.* My first impression of Mrs. Van was that she was very loud because she talked a lot more compared to Mrs. O. Mrs. O was a quiet and shy kind of lady. I had no idea the impact or importance that Mrs. Van would become in my life. It's like what the Bible verse Matthew 7:1 says, "Judge not, that you be not judged."

(Rabbit trail. Behavior is the key to show God's love and how much you changed to others. As followers of Christ, we are called to act differently because we are His stewards. In love, direct people, not force them to God. Don't let your opinion ruin something. Embrace the situation and the outcome may surprise you!)

5th Grade Getaway

The month of April had evolved and the fifth grade class went on a three-day camping trip to Grad Hill where everybody slept in log cabins on the floor. My mom came along to take care of me. Mrs. Van, my mom, and I had a golf cart there to move from place-to-place. I was in charge of making it go. Sometimes I would go really fast while somebody steered it, which was really fun!

On the first day there, Mrs. Van, my mom, and I went canoeing. I sat in the middle on the floor of it. My pants were soaked from the water that Mrs. Van and my mom got in it and I was kind of cold from my wet pants, the water, and the wind. When we returned to the canoeing launch site, Mrs. O was standing and waiting for us. I was real excited to see her. I hugged her really tight with my wet pants and life jacket on, which hurt when I was hugging her, but I kept hugging anyway.

My mom and I went to our cabin to change into a dry pair of jeans. Then we went to the beach and sat on a blanket in the sand and talked to Mrs. O and Mrs. Van. Then all of us tie-died our T-shirts. After they were dry, we wore them and had somebody take our picture. We sat on a bench with a barn and the sun behind us. I am in the middle of Mrs. Van and Mrs. O with my mom standing behind me. The photo turned out to be one of my favorite memories.

(Rabbit trail. Live simply, love generously, care deeply, and speak kindly. For we walk by faith and not by sight! Cherish yesterday, dream tomorrow, and live for today! Focus on God's blessings in your life. A friend is someone who reaches for your hand, but touches your heart.)

A Dream Come True

When I was 15 years old, I went to a Heidi Day concert in July. I was crazy about her. I had everything that a teenage girl could have that had to do with Heidi Day. My mom bought tickets to her concert and she tried to have me meet Heidi Day, but had no luck. So Mrs. Van tried without me knowing about it. Of course, I met her and in October, I received a package from her sponsors called the Meet & Greet Group. I received: a CD, T-shirt, socks, pillow, sunglasses, keychain, and a card. I kept it all. Listen to my story about it.

June 2005, I arrived home off the bus and my mom said, "Emily, guess who is coming to the Van Andel?" I looked at her with a confused look and asked, "Who?" My mom said, "Heidi Day!! It was on the TV and I'm going to try to get tickets!" I said, "That would be SO COOL if you can get tickets. My dream would come early if I could go to one of her concerts. Remember I wanted to go to one for my sweet 16th birthday gift?" She said, "I know. I'm going to try my hardest. The concert is July 20."

The next day I told Mrs. Van all that my mom had told me. Mrs. Van said, "Oh, wouldn't that be cool if your mom can get tickets?" I was smiling from ear-to-ear and said, "Yes." Mrs. Van said, "What would be even cooler is if she could get you to see and meet Heidi Day." I said, "I know!"

When I arrived home that night, my mom said that she got tickets, but had no luck on getting a chance to meet Heidi Day. I was still excited that I was going.

When I told Mrs. Van, the news that my mom got the tickets, but had no luck in getting the chance to meet Heidi Day, Mrs. Van said, "Well I'll try then." I exclaimed, "MRS. VAN NO!" My mom tried and she got nowhere. So I thought that it was pointless and hopeless for Mrs. Van to try also.

Dimly Lit

The last day of school had come and Mrs. Van and I said our goodbyes to each other. We hugged and did not talk about the concert.

Summer had begun and Mrs. Van and I kept each other updated on how and what we were doing over the summer like usual. Well, little did I know that she was making phone calls to the Meet & Greet club for Heidi Day. She kept getting closed doors about me being able to meet Heidi Day in person. She called everyone everywhere. What kept her going was that "MRS. VAN NO!" She also had to write a couple of letters about me and had a couple people from the administration building write letters. This situation reminded me of Mathew 7:7-8 which says, "Ask and it will be given to you; seek and you will find; knock and the door will be opened to you. For everyone who asks receives; he who seeks finds; and to him who knocks, the door will be opened."

July 19, 2005, the phone rang so my mom went outside on the porch to talk with a pen and a

Dimly Lit

pad of paper. I could see her talking and laughing while I was watching TV. When the music video to Heidi Day's ""Wake Up"" song came on, I turned the volume way up to dance and sing along. Finally, my mom came in and I asked, "Who was that on the phone?" She said, "Oh a customer that I didn't want Dad to know about because I didn't want to do the job." I believed that, but later, I found out that it was really Mrs. Van giving my mom the info on what she had to do the next night at the concert.

The day of the Heidi Day concert had finally arrived! July 20, 2005! I woke up early and couldn't sleep in because I was excited for the concert. I was good and didn't bug my mom about the concert all day, which many people think that I did, but I didn't. I just played around on my computer and listened to Heidi Day songs.

My dad came home from work and that meant that it was finally time to get ready for the concert. I was only waiting for that time ALL DAY!

I changed into my T-shirt that said "Heidi's Best Friend."

On the way to the Van Andel, we popped in a CD of Heidi Day, of course. When we reached the parking lot, my mom was kind of hurrying and telling my dad to park there and there and there, but my dad didn't listen. That made my mom a little mad. I said, "Mom, calm down. We will get there. Don't worry."

When we were walking to the doors, the excitement grew and when I was inside, the excitement grew even more! We had to wait in line for the box office and when it was our turn, my dad and I stood back while my mom went up and talked to the guy. A few minutes went by. She came back and put on a red bracelet around my wrist. While putting it on, she said, "You are going to see Heidi Day," I thought: *Yeah I know. That's why we are here.*

Standing in line to meet Heidi Day, I was clueless to what was happening. Getting closer to

Dimly Lit

the doors and when my mom and I were inside of the room, we were greeted by Roy (Heidi's body guard). He was nice and joked around with me about my T-shirt. He said, "Nice shirt. Heidi is going to love your shirt when she sees it." I just smiled.

I was the fourth person in line to meet Heidi Day out of 84. When Roy was getting everybody to be quiet, he shouted, "EVERYBODY CAN I HAVE YOUR ATTENTION! CAN I HAVE EVERYBODY'S ATTENTION PLEASE! OK, thank you. OK, I'm going to bring Heidi Day out, but she can only take pictures. No autographs because she is crunched for time. There are eighty-four of you so you have to be fast and keep moving so she can see all of you. Don't ask her for her autograph and if you do, then the next person in line won't meet her. And we don't want that. We want everybody to meet her that's here now. OK? Alright. Now I'm going to bring out Heidi."

The excitement built in everyone and when we all saw Heidi Day, everybody screamed! When it was my turn to meet her, Roy motioned me to come up. He said to Heidi, "Heidi, don't you just love her shirt?" Heidi said, "Aw! I love it!" as she touched my arm with her cold fingers. We took the picture and I went out the doors. I screamed when I was out of that room and from that moment on, I was on cloud nine!

On the way home, I said to my mom, "Mom, my dream of meeting Heidi Day and going to her concert came true and early!"

My mom told me what Mrs. Van did the next day. I called her and thanked her, wrote her an e-mail, and my mom and I told her about the night.

It was once in lifetime opportunity and something that I'll NEVER forget!

(Rabbit trail. Think of children, and when they admire a celebrity and purchase every merchandise product they run across. Or this may be you with a loved one in your life. You may even be obsessed with this person that you cannot see his or her flaws. Obsessing over celebrities or loved ones can become idols. You may have put them first instead of putting God as your number One. I understand this first hand because I have done it. I even was at the extent of talking to imaginary friends because I didn't have friends who were my age in my life.)

We Thought They'd Never End

Ding a ling was the sound of the school's bell that brought me back to reality from daydreaming. I blinked three times to come back to the sense of the boring school day. My face jerked away from my tingling hand, which it was resting on. It had fallen asleep. Racing through the halls, I was trying to get to the cafeteria as fast as a mountain lion. The problem was other students were dragging their feet going slow, as if they were old grandmas and grandpas walking with walkers. Finally, I reached the cafeteria and I could see that I beat my friends to the table. I started unpacking my lunch as my friends, like little robots, started taking their normal seats. My best friend, Alicia, sat down next to me and made small talk asking things like, "How are you?" and "How is your day going so far?"

Our four pack of friends sat gabbing away. You know that is what girls do best. Nikki, a girl who talks with her hands, is so bubbly. She has brown eyes and long blonde hair that she wears in a ponytail. She is really close with a girl named Chelsea who has blue eyes and long wavy hair. She is a girly girl and is always glancing at her face in the mirror that is in her purse to fix her hair. Everything has to be picture perfect with her. Her lips are shaped like a sombrero hat and her teeth look like chipmunk teeth. Alicia is just like me, in being a tomboy, but wearing girly jeans. She has dark brown eyes. You could say when looking at them, it's like looking at a chocolate lake. Her brown hair is long and she wears it in a ponytail. Nikki blurted out, "Yeah, Alicia is moving to Arizona." I exclaimed, "WHAT?!" My face painted with confusion when looking at her and then to Alicia.

    Luckily, Mrs. Van showed up and slid in her normal seat in the cafeteria next to me so she could feed me. She said, "What's going on?"

I replied, "Oh, Alicia is moving to Arizona." in a cocky attitude. Now I'm getting a little fired up because of the news I just found out.

Mrs. Van reached behind herself to pull the back of her shirt down and said to Alicia, "What? You are?" with a confused expression on her face. Alicia answered with a nod and a "Yes."

Mrs. Van replied, "Why are you moving to Arizona? What's out there? Do you have family out there?" Alicia answered, "Because my mom wants to and no, we don't have family out there." Mrs. Van replied, "Oh, OK." with her face resting on her hand making her words muffled a bit. Scratching her nose and clearing her throat, she said, "Do you personally want to move to Arizona? If you have a choice to move, would you?" looking at Alicia straight in the eye. Alicia answered, "No, I want to stay here with all of my friends." Mrs. Van replied, "That is understandable, Alicia. Every kid your age would say the same thing you just said." with a grin. Alicia just smiled.

After lunch, I felt like I was in a daze or a trance because I could not believe that Alicia, my best friend, the person who sees past my disability, was moving in a week. *My buddy, my pal, oh, why are you leaving? Why...why...why.* I did what 1 Peter 5:6-7 says to do, which states, "Humble yourselves, therefore, under the mighty hand of God so that at the proper time he may exalt you, casting all your anxieties on him, because he cares for you."

After school, Alicia and I always talked when waiting for the arrival for Alicia's bus. That day Alicia asked, "Em, are you OK?"

I replied, "Yeah. Why?" I was scrunching my eyebrows up at her. She replied, "Because I really wanted to tell you in private, I didn't know that Nikki and her big mouth would have told you at lunch today." I replied, "Oh Alicia, it is fine. Don't worry about it." I was trying to console her, but deep down, I was a little disappointed.

When I arrived home that day, I knew that she was leaving in a week, so I started cracking and spitting out words on my computer, writing all of the memories down that we have been through since the seventh grade. I wrote thoughts that I have had of us, looking forward to going to each others' open houses and being each other's maid of honor in our weddings. Also I thanked her for being such a good friend.

The time had come, Alicia's last day at our school. I gave my gift to her in the morning because she was standing in the hall by the front entrance gabbing away to her friend. Plus, I didn't want to be carrying it all day until lunch. I handed her the card that I had the letter I wrote in it and said, "Here open this and read it when you have time." She nodded and said, "OK." looking at me with those dark brown eyes of hers and her chubby cheeks.

At lunchtime, we had a pizza party planned for Alicia. Mrs. Van had her camera along, which at first didn't work, but then it did. When it wasn't working I thought: *Yes!* Because I don't like being in pictures and I don't know why. Alicia arrived to lunch late. After lunch, she pulled me aside to ask me if I was OK. I shook my head and said, "Yes." trying not to cry.

At the end of the day, the time had come where Alicia and I had to say our good-byes to each other. When Alicia reached me she had her gift from me: pink balloons and her backpack. She showed me her pictures that were in her locker and she gave me one to keep. All around us, I could hear lockers slamming shut, murmurs of students talking to their friends, and announcements over the speaker. Alicia's bus had arrived and she gave me a long hug. While hugging, I smelled her hair and when we pulled away I gave her a smile. As I watched her walk away, I felt like everything went into slow motion. Even the bus driving away seemed to be a blur.

All things pass, some people might say. It is true. My feelings of loneness and sadness, because of not seeing or talking to Alicia in person every day have passed. So I know it is hard at first, but there's always a light at the end of the tunnel. The Bible verse of 1 Peter 5:10 popped in my head, which says, "And after you have suffered a little while, the God of all grace, who has called you to his eternal glory in Christ, will himself restore, confirm, strengthen, and establish you."

(Rabbit trail. In life, there are circumstances that people do not want to or cannot imagine going through. It is easy to be dependent on others. A person can be too reliant that he or she does not think that he or she can live without this person. This person can lead the friend into bad behaviors. Sometimes certain relationships can be hinders. One person can be smothering the other person. The reaction of this is the person distancing himself or herself at arms length from the smothering person. Time and space are needed for people to change and mature. Separation can be good. Behavior is the key to show love and how much you changed to others.)

First Boyfriend

I was in my junior year of high school and I had two classes with Darren the year before so I kind of knew him, but liked him as just a friend. Somehow he came over on a Friday night and we watched *The Phantom of the Opera*. That was the stupidest movie that I have ever seen. Afterwards Darren asked, "Did you like the movie?" "Yes." I said. The next week of school, whenever I saw Darren in the halls, I felt nervous and excited at the same time so I thought: *OK. What is going on? Why am I feeling this way?* On Saturday, Darren and I were chatting online for a couple of hours and somewhere in the middle I asked him to date me. I said, " Darren, do you want to date me and be like girlfriend and boyfriend?" A Pause. "Em, I would LOVE TO! I have liked you since last year.'" he said. "You have?" "YES!" he said.

Darren changed his relationship status online what seemed like a few seconds after we established we were going out together. I smiled and more excitement built up inside of me.

In the beginning of our relationship, I would sneak away from Mrs. Van to meet Darren by the library so I could give him a hug and talk for a couple of minutes before I headed up to my study hour. Finally, I told Mrs. Van what I was doing because I was sneaking around. She said, "Oh, I don't care if you go to see and hug Darren after I get you done with the bathroom. He's your boyfriend. You should be doing that anyways." I giggled and smiled at her. I felt relieved after I told her.

So Darren and I met up at our meeting place and some days he wasn't there. Some days we would have notes for each other. When Valentine's Day rolled around, I was one lucky girl. I was a few minutes late in meeting Darren at the library, but it was a really good thing. As I zipped by the corner, I saw Darren standing with his arms full of gifts. My mouth dropped open and I covered it. He bought me flowers, balloons, a bag of M&M's, and crafted a homemade card.

    Darren and I went to the Snowball dance together. That day we communicated by instant message to each other like we normally did until we had to get ready. I was ready and had to wait for him to arrive. I was cold because that is how I get when I am nervous. Also I had butterflies in my stomach. When he arrived, he gave me a mushy card and then we took pictures.

    After an hour of that, my mom and her friend, Linda, drove us to Italian Garden for supper. We had a 35-minute wait for our table. So Darren stood that entire amount of time. When we received our food, Darren fed me because my disability will not allow me to feed myself. He blew on my food to make it cooler and at first it was sweet of him to do. Then he continued to blow when I knew it wasn't hot anymore and it got annoying after a while. I said that I was full, but I wasn't really because I knew that it was getting close when the dance started and I was getting pretty annoyed by his slowness.

On the way to the dance, it was snowing really hard and my mom does not like to drive in snow. So it was a quiet ride there and when we arrived, Darren and I had a blast! He took me out of my wheelchair when slow songs played to dance like an able-bodied couple dances. While we were dancing like that I could feel my heart pulsating really fast. At one point, I kissed him on his cheek because I just felt like it was the perfect time. Darren had to sit down a lot by the DJ when fast songs played. He said that it was from dancing, but I think it was from him standing for 35-minutes at Italian Garden. So we only danced to the slow songs.

The dance was let out early because of the snow was coming down really bad and you could barely see while driving. My dad picked us up and we had to take Darren home.

Dimly Lit

Darren and I had been dating for three months and he invited me to his house for Easter. Darren's sister and her family were there also. I had gone to my church with my parents and the service went longer than expected. When I arrived to Darren's house, I could tell that he was anxious about me arriving later than expected.

We small talked before lunch was ready. I talked to his brother-in-law who was asking me several questions about school, and myself and by this, he made me feel at ease. Everyone ate lunch and afterwards Darren told me that he wanted some alone time with me. At the time, I was playing with his little nieces and nephew, and so I excused myself. Darren brought me to his room and shut the door so his nephew would not come in. I felt uncomfortable. We took pictures, talked and listened to CDs. A few hours later we decided to go downstairs to watch *High School Musical.*

While we were watching the movie, I kept looking at him a lot. The kids were running up and down the stairs so it was noisy. Finally he said, "What?" I said, "You know what." He looked at me with a confused look. I just smiled. A few minutes later he said, "Oh. You want a kiss.'" with a grin. I laughed nervously and said, "Yes!" A few hours later we kissed and it was my first kiss.

I was at Darren's house for most of the day, even though I hadn't planned on being there so long. The day flew by so quickly. By the end of the night, my instincts could sense that Darren's parents were ready for me to go home.

In May, Darren and I went to Prom together. It was his senior year and my junior year for Prom. We had been dating for four months at that time. It was a school day and the Prom was at night, which was stupid because many students were absent because they were getting ready for Prom. The weather was rainy all day and we had planned to take pictures at a park with another couple, but instead we took them in my house. Darren and I took many without the other couple. The rain had stopped so we took a couple outside. Then we had to wait for them to show up. Then we took more pictures with them and ate supper, which was lasagna.

We drove in separate cars to the Prom spot. Once there, we met up again and danced the night away! More pictures were taken with friends. At first, Darren went to the punch bowl a lot, and I went with him twice. After that, I let him go by himself because I did not want the dance to end. I was having a blast! I could tell that Darren was unsure how to dance, but by the end of the night, he was comfortable dancing and having fun also.

After the Prom, it was still raining cats and dogs. Then we went to an after party at a friend's house. There we ate chocolate chip cookie dough that I loved. A few people played games when we waiting for people to show up. Then we watched an episode of *The Office*.

My parents and I had to take Darren home and we didn't get home until one-thirty in the morning.

Two weeks after Prom, I broke up with Darren on a Saturday night on instant messenger because I didn't have feelings for him anymore. Also, I didn't like what he taught me to do. I have always talked out my problems and he kept his inside of him. I was beginning to do that and I didn't like that so I broke up with him two weeks before his graduation. Boy that was a mistake because he talked bad about me, ruining my good reputation! His mom even called my mom one day to see why and what happened, and if they could put us back together. I was so upset when I heard his mom had called, so I answered my mom's questions in an upset tone.

At school, I received the famous break up question, "Are you OK?" I told people that I was fine and was the one who broke it off. Darren was saying that it was mutual, but I told them that I had ended it. Those few weeks of school were terrible, and I looked forward to summer all the more.

(Rabbit trail. In high school, many students think that dating is fun and will be with significant other for the rest of their lives. At that age, students are immature and tend to not have the knowledge of how to make dating relationships work or last. Once a significant other makes the decision to breakup the dating relationship because of the negatives outweigh the positives, they should stick to it because they are right! People need to listen to their hearts more often because it seems to be always correct. Sometimes people cannot change others.

God has taught me not to awaken love until it desires. So ladies, wait for men to ask you out and don't play the flirt game. The flirt game gets you nowhere and gets you disappointed or mad. Take 1st Corinthians 7:32-35 to heart as I did and continue to, as Paul is speaking to the Corinthians, which states, "I would like you to be free from concern. An unmarried man is concerned about the

Lord's affairs—how he can please the Lord. But a married man is concerned about the affairs of this world—how he can please his wife— and his interests are divided. An unmarried woman or virgin is concerned about the Lord's affairs: Her aim is to be devoted to the Lord in both body and spirit. But a married woman is concerned about the affairs of this world—how she can please her husband. I am saying this for your own good, not to restrict you, but that you may live in a right way in undivided devotion to the Lord." See how being single is positive because of the focus is on our desire in following God in everything!)

School's Out for Summer

The day before the last day of my junior year was awesome! First of all, I started my exams on Monday because it takes me longer to take them. So Monday, I finished my first hour exam, which felt really good to get it done. On Tuesday, I started my third hour exam and finished that by the end of the day. I felt like I did well on it so Mrs. Van said that I didn't need to study that night. Wednesday rolled around and she said that it was going to be a goof-off and fun day for us because I was so far ahead on my exams than the rest of the students. They had Wednesday and Thursday to get theirs done and Thursday was a half-day. So she said that I was going to walk in my walker (for exercise), try to send some pictures to my e-mail, study for French Culture exam, and go to Cheddar's for a shake. Well, we did three out of the four things that day and guess what one we didn't do? Study for French Culture! Wednesday was SO much fun and

Mrs. Van kept saying, "This is going to be a fun day! You have no clue!" over and over again. We both laughed when she said that.

Lunchtime rolled around and I thought that Mr. Van was going to bring in dessert pizza from Stable Ranch by what Mrs. Van had said, but that was just a guess. So I didn't eat that much, but when Mrs. Van said, "No, you need to eat because it's not what you think it is."

So I ate and I had to go to the bathroom REALLY BAD for some reason that day! Mrs. Van said, "No. Just wait for ten more minutes." as she was looking at her watch.

I think I only gave her five then I wheeled to the bathroom as fast as I could! When I reached the door, I hit the door handle to see if it were unlocked. And nope, it wasn't! When I turned around to see how far back Mrs. Van was behind me, I saw ALICIA STANDING THERE! I couldn't believe it Alicia my best friend, the one who moved to Arizona in January 2007. I kept in touch with her by e-mailing her. OH MY GOSH I COULDN'T BELIEVE IT! Mrs. Van and Alicia said that my eyes looked like they were going to pop out. My face turned white as a ghost they said. I hugged Alicia then I went to the bathroom.

In the bathroom, I was speechless and I think I didn't look at Mrs. Van. On the toilet, I couldn't go because of all the excitement! Finally, I went and asked Mrs. Van, "Is this real? Is she real?" She said, "Yes, she is!"

I wheeled out of the bathroom. I hugged Alicia again and we just talked from 10:40 A.M. to 2:45 P.M. We went to the library and talked while Mrs. Van ate her lunch, but we were loud so Mrs. Van put us in a room and shut the door. Alicia and I kept on talking away. We took some pictures with Alicia's camera. I showed her the story that I wrote about her moving away.

After Mrs. Van finished eating, all three of us went and found Alicia's old teachers that she wanted to talk to. Then we went to Cheddar's with

Ana, another friend of Alicia's and mine, for shakes. We talked while we walked there and back. Then we arrived back to school. Alicia wanted to talk to some more of her teachers and find Kameron. So we did that and Mrs. Van went home sometime, I don't know when, because she didn't say good-bye. And when I went back to her office to say good-bye at two fifty-five, she was gone. So all day I was on cloud nine! I wasn't in the mood to study for my French Culture exam that night right away, but after the excitement wore off, and reality set in, I did.

So my first day of summer vacation, I had Alicia over all day! I showed her all of my journals that were about her that I wrote in Creative Writing. We took lots of pictures. She showed me her yearbook. We watched *High School Musical 2* and *Where the Heart Is*. We ate lunch and went for a walk. On our way back, we were caught in a rain shower and that was sort of fun. We played games and ate supper. It was SO much fun! The next

Dimly Lit

Wednesday Mrs. Van, Alicia, and I went out for ice cream at the "Zondlak's" ice cream place. It was Alicia's birthday on Thursday so we kind of got together for that reason. On Friday, Alicia wanted to have a sleepover with me. She left on the 28th of June, which was such a short time to spend with her. It made me kind of sad.

June 18, 2008, Mrs. Van, Alicia, and I had a good time getting ice cream and we talked every moment along the way. Ana came along, and brought her little sister too. I gave Alicia her birthday present. I bought her best friends necklaces and a card that sang. She let me wear the best half heart one and she wore the friends' part. We took pictures and Alicia showed us her pictures from last week when she went to her cousin's Open House.

On June 22, 2008, Alicia's and my sleepover was fun! When she came to my house on Friday, she brought a wasp into the house so my mom said to us, "Watch it while I go get the fly swatter." But you know what best friends do when they are together, they talk and that's what we did instead of watching the wasp. It took two-hours before my mom saw and killed it.

We went outside and watched Gerrit and Jack (my neighbors) swim for a little bit. We took pictures outside then we went back inside because it was hot out. Alicia checked her e-mail then she wanted Darren to come over just to hang out with us. We instant messaged him and had a good time with that. Even though Darren and I were not a couple, we still are friends. My mom said that it was time to go at two o'clock and my dad took a half-day off from work so he went with us also. We went to the movie place and rented four movies. Also we went to the bank, the grocery store to get munches, and we ate at Happy Place for lunch. Then we watched –well, Alicia made me watch, *Happily Never Ever After*, which I thought was going to be lame because it was a cartoon, but it was OK. Then we called Darren to bug him about coming over, but he couldn't because he had a bonfire to go to. Then we instant messaged him for a while. We ate supper and Alicia talked to Darren again after. Then we had a fire with my mom, Dad, and Gerrit. Of course, we had s'mores. We took pictures with Gerrit by the fire eating s'mores with chocolate all over his face.

Then we began to get ready for the night and changed into our PJs while Alicia talked to Darren again on instant messenger. We watched *I Am Reed* movie and ate candy. The movie was good, but it was slow it seemed like to me. We went to bed around two o'clock in the morning, but I didn't. I finally fell asleep around four-thirty. I had strange anxiety over all the communication between Darren and Alicia. I thought her continuously wanting to instant message him was kind of strange, since she had only heard about him through my stories of dating him and that we are still friends.

On June 26, 2008, it was just Mrs. Van, Alicia, and I that went for ice cream, which was nice. Alicia had said that she wanted Darren to come with us, but he didn't. I had a stomachache and had only five hours of sleep the night before so I wasn't my normal happy talkative self. The reason why I only had five hours of sleep was because I was stressing about the possibility of seeing him again. We talked over e-mails and instant messaged, but that was the only communication we had since we broke up. It was nice to visit with Alicia again, but it was time for her to go back to Arizona.

    (Rabbit trail. After I made the decision to live for Jesus Christ, God began to work on me about the unforgiveness that I had stored up in my heart. I didn't want to forgive others who had hurt me. I didn't listen to God. Let me tell you when God tells you to do something, obey because He will keep nudging and reminding you to do it. God kept nudging and reminding through His Word and other things, such as praise songs and conversations. He will use whatever He wants. He taught me that the feelings that I have against my loved ones would be the same feelings He would have about me and would behave the same way toward me as I was acting toward others. I wasn't doing anything to them by holding onto grudges. I was hurting myself and stopping God's plan for my journey.)

† † †

Looking back on my childhood, I certainly did learn valuable lessons that I still remember today. Honesty, even though it may be hard, is the best policy. Friendship is a continuous garden with all types of wild flowers in it that is continuously growing. The deep seeds that flourish year after year are your true friends for life. The experiences I have had throughout my life, I would not have traded for anything. Just a reminder of the golden rule, "Treat others as you want to be treated." Remember, just because other people look different, like disabled people do, does not mean they are dumb or any different than you.

Tragic Senior Year

September 24, 2008

Well, my senior year of high school ISN'T going like I thought it was going to be! GRRRR! Mrs. Van and I are ONLY together for two hours as well as lunch a day. You know the famous saying, "Your senior year is your best year ever!" Well, so far, that saying is FALSE! Mrs. Van works with another Special Ed class while I attend my four classes by myself. I know I said that I wanted my independence, but this is not what I imagined it would be like! The grass ISN'T greener on the other side! I am depressed, but I act like everything is fine! My saying is for this year has to be "roll with the punches." Even though I DON'T WANT TO! Think about it, how would you feel if your best friend "left" you after being right-by-your-side for nine years? I have cried for four weeks at night because I feel like nobody understands what I'm feeling.

October 19, 2008

I signed up to play Powder Puff a couple weeks earlier. But first, I e-mailed the principal to see if I could play and if it were OK for a disabled person to play. Well, he said, "Yes!" He came in and talked to me while I was in my resource hour with Mrs. Engel. I didn't tell her that I e-mailed Mr. Fern and asked. So when he was talking to us, she had no clue what we were talking about. Mr. Fern just assumed that I talked to Mrs. Engel first and then e-mailed him. But nope, I didn't. I am taking the word "independence" seriously. After our discussion, Mrs. Engel told me that she was proud of me.

So I went to all of the practices and talked to the coach through e-mail for a few weeks before the big game.

Finally, the game day arrived, and it was raining off and on throughout the day. Mr. Fern told me that I couldn't play at the game that night because the field was too muddy for my wheelchair.

I was bummed when I heard the news because my team had a special play just for me to do.

My mom dressed me in my uniform because I was going to support my team even though I couldn't play. Our coach wanted us, players, to arrive at the school's practice field to practice one more time. I sat out for some of the practice because I knew I wasn't playing, so why practice?

While sitting and watching my teammates running plays, Mrs. Engel showed up and talked to me a little bit. I asked her to stand by me during the game to keep me company. Then she left to go to the field. A few minutes went by and I hear a shout. "EMILY ZONDLAK!" I whipped my head around and it was my sister, Ashley, who shouted! I rode by her and talked to her for a few minutes. Ashley surprised my family and I because nobody said she would come because she was in college in Alma. I was excited to see her!

The game starts and Mrs. Engel explains the game to me a little bit because I had no idea what

Dimly Lit 77

was happening. I only signed up to play because I wanted to make my senior year my best year ever, even though it wasn't going that way. When my senior teammates scored against the juniors, I cheered and got the crowd excited. I saw that Mrs. Van came when I cheered at some point. I was happy that she came because I didn't invite her. The reason why I didn't was because I didn't want to make her come if she didn't want to. I was making myself pull away from her because of the famous "independence" word this year.

    At some point during the game, Mr. Black ran up to me to say that I was going to play! I was so excited! He pushed my wheelchair while I steered with my control so I wouldn't get my wheelchair stuck. I had to wait for a few minutes on the field. So Mr. Black and Mr. Runners joked with me. While they did, I heard the crowd chanting my name! Their cheers made me feel even more excited in wanting to do my play. A few minutes went by and I finally got to do my play! When I got the ball, my teammates blocked the juniors so Mr. Black and I could do my play. We drove the football seven yards!

Getting off the field, I was so happy and everybody was cheering for me! Then Mr. Black wanted me to follow him so he could wash my tires off. Mrs. Engel helped us do that. Then a little while later, the game was done and we, the seniors, won! Then everybody took tons of pictures in the mud!

I had my mom send flowers to Mr. Black along with my thank-you note because of what he did.

February 2, 2009

Mrs. Engel was told that there was a full-ride scholarship opportunity and that a few teachers nominated me for it. I thought that was cool and wanted to try to receive it. She told me that one student out of every state would be applying. All I had to do was answer these questions. The questions were:

1. Which degree/program are you interested in pursuing?

2. How will a University of Phoenix education help you achieve your career/ personal/ life goals?

3. What obstacles or challenges have you overcome/ will you face in order to complete your education?

Here was my entry:

I am interested in pursuing an Associate of Arts in Hospitality, Travel and Tourism and an Associate of Arts in Communications. These online courses would help me to achieve my career goal of becoming an author. I have found that I have enjoyed expressing myself through my words. For the major part of my life, I have kept a journal where I began to write about my personal experiences. That was what led me to start imagining becoming a writer. I also enjoy writing short stories and have written articles for my high school newspaper. (Rabbit trail. I attained my

Associates of Arts with a Concentration in Communications and my Bachelor of Arts in English.)

A University of Phoenix education will help me achieve my career/ personal/ life goals by expressing my feelings in black and white on paper. I always imagined going to college, but after pursuing some college visits, I knew that going to college and living in the dorms was not a possibility anymore so I looked at online colleges. Taking these online courses, I will be in my barrier-free environment and I will not be judged for my disability or by other students. This will help me achieve my career goals and potentially make me a better writer.

An obstacle or a challenge I will face in order to complete my education is mobility around college campuses, which would be difficult for me especially in the winter months because of my power wheelchair. Also, study pace would be an obstacle or challenge because I will not be

Dimly Lit

considered a full-time student while taking one course at a time. Online education courses would allow me to take my time on a course instead of stressing over taking and finishing several courses at once. As a nonverbal student, another obstacle or challenge I have in order to complete my education would be communicating with others. Taking online courses will not be a challenge because I communicate the best through my writing.

I would like to express my gratitude for being considered for the potential scholarship opportunity that this would provide me with my future education.

(Rabbit trail. God taught me that He strengthens me! God is faithful! He kept molding and transforming me to glorify Him! I'm thankful on what He has done and spending time to make me new! Jesus Christ made and will continue to make me into a new person! God makes all things possible for those who have a fully devoted heart with a love desiring for Him! I always wanted to attend college, but never thought it would be online. It's like what God's Word says, we make our plans, but the Lord directs our footsteps! God planned this journey and brought it into completion!)

March 1, 2009

Even though my senior year isn't going like I pictured it would, I am having a great year outside of school! That is one plus! My family is hanging out and going to fun places more! I love it when I get to see my Uncle Mark, Aunt Amy, Brooke, Luke, Trevor, Aunt Nay Nay, Aunt Connie, Oompa, and G more!

March 10, 2009

I woke up around 8:30 A.M. on my day off from school. The seniors had the day off because the juniors had to take the MME test because that is what you do when you are a junior. The only people, who were allowed to be in school with them, were the teachers.

I started my day off figuring out why my college writing BYU class was not working on my school laptop. I went through the intro part of the class and then my mom called me to eat breakfast. She made me a bowl of Maple and Brown Sugar Oatmeal and two warm strawberry pop tarts. Suddenly, the phone rang. It was Aunt Amy wanting to know if I wanted Cheddar's for breakfast. Of course, I said, "Yes! So Aunt Amy arrived at our house to watch and hang out with me while my parents are at work.

Aunt Amy, my mom, and I started to chit-chat because that is what ladies do when they are together and have not seen one another for a while. So Aunt Amy starts feeding me my sandwich and chocolate shake while she and my mom were still chitchatting. Then my mom has to leave for work. So Aunt Amy and I keep eating, talking, and laughing.

We played card games like Slap Jack and War. Aunt Amy said that I cheated at War, but how can you at that game? Then we found my Uno Attack game, but it did not work so we put it back.

Then we went through all of my photo albums that I have in my room. I was hungry again so Aunt Amy heated up my half of sandwich from Cheddar's and a bag of popcorn. Then my dad came home and Aunt Amy left. My dad and I did our normal routine.

March 11, 2009

My mom woke me up because I had a half-day since MME testing is going on this week at school. I woke up at 4:00 A.M. for some odd reason. I stayed awake for an hour and thankfully, I fell back asleep, otherwise, I would have been very upset. Then my mom woke me up at 10:00 A.M. to get ready for my half-day of school. She warmed up what I was about to eat yesterday before Aunt Amy called. Then I got dressed. On the way to school, my mom popped in *A Walk to Remember* CD and we turned the volume up way loud. We danced and sang along to our favorite song.

When I arrived at school, I did my normal thing, but supposedly, Mrs. Van had it in her mind to help me get my coat off. I didn't know that. So I asked one of the teacher aides to help me with it. One of them said that Mrs. Van was up there looking for me. I had a confused look on my face. A few minutes later, Mrs. Van showed up and asked if I came up the normal way I usually took. I said, "Yes." She explained to me what she did and asked me a few questions. I said, "Yes." to all of them. I knew and could tell that she was stressed out and uneasy so I gave her a huge hug.

March 12, 2009

My mom woke me up because I had my senior breakfast at school so I did not eat at home. Then I got dressed. On the way to school, my mom popped in *A Walk to Remember* CD and we turned the volume up way loud. We danced and sang alone to our favorite song like we did yesterday. My mom is protective of me and she wanted to open up the school doors for me. I said, "No Mom. I got it. I can do it myself. I am a big girl!" with some giggles in between. I went to the cafeteria and on the way there, I peeked in the room where Mrs. Van usually is when she is not helping me. The lights were off and of course, she was not in there. So I just kept on my path toward the cafeteria. Once I reached there, I sat my gloves down and got in line to receive my graduation cap and gown stuff. When I received it, I went back and sat down at a table. I moved from three different tables just to sit by my close group of friends.

The food was OK and I also won a gift card to Mac's & Erma's by a raffle ticket. Mrs. Jumpy told us to try on our caps and gowns, and to hang them up so that if they did not fit, the people could fix them. Also, it will get the wrinkles out so that our moms do not have to iron it.

March 13, 2009

I had a full day of school, but it was an easy day. First hour, I walked (for exercise) without Mrs. Van, which was kind of fun because some teachers and janitors teased me about silly stuff. While I was walking and not bothered by anyone, I thought about Mrs. Van and how she is doing OK with our new situation, which makes me really happy. I was a little nervous and worried about how she would react, but she seems to be doing fine. This trimester is like the first where we are only together for two hours every day in the morning. In the beginning of the school year that was so difficult for us because we were used to being together all day, but this year is about my independence. That was a wake-up call. No matter if I wanted it or not, I got it. Whoa man, it was difficult, and during the summer months, I usually would cry every now and then because that was how much I missed her. But I didn't cry at all this past summer. I made it up big time in the first three weeks of school because a couple of times a week, I cried at night in bed. It felt like I was going through a break up and I kind of was.

    While gliding and Mrs. Van walking beside me, I said, "I'm so happy that you are happy." She asked, "What do you mean?" "Oh nothing." I said because I knew if I told her what I meant she would be sad. I didn't and don't want that.

I had an easy day at school and a busy weekend ahead. How did that work out? That seems not right to me, but oh well.

March 14, 2009

I wrote my movie reflection for World Lit and that's hard to write a full page without double spacing. So I have a cartoon in the middle of the page filling up half of the page. I hope Mr. Hair thinks it is great! Some people might say that is cheating, but shh, don't tell Mr. Hair that! I selected which creation myth that I am doing a presentation on next week. Some of the myths that I found and read were crazy. Of course, I picked the shortest one to do out of my six that I found. I felt so lame because at first, I was typing all out on my own and finding pictures to go with each slide. I had done four slides when I realized that I had it saved on my laptop so I can just copy and paste it. I felt so lame and thought: *Why didn't I think of this sooner? GRR!*

I received my report card from last trimester in the mail. My mom, dad, and I are so happy about my good grades, so my dad said; "We are going to go Mac's & Erma's to celebrate your good grades and your scholarship after church." I received a full-ride scholarship to University of Phoenix for four years. It was after church, and my mom forgot to bring along her purse and I forgot my 10 dollars gift card at home. So, we went home. I thought that we were not going because we had to go home first, but nope, we went after all. The food was horrible and I was still hungry! My mom said to me in the bathroom stall, "We are not eating here ever again." I read a sign that was in the bathroom that said, "Great food. Great memories." I said, "Yeah right!" to the great food part of it.

March 15, 2009

I woke up two minutes before noon and I thought: *Uh-oh. Dad will tease me about waking up at noon.* I knocked on the wall and I said to Dad, "It's still morning Dad." He said, "I know, you are right." with a grinned. He has teased me a little bit, but nothing bad this time, thankfully.

Aunt Nay Nay called to talk and figure out which day she is coming this week. I thought: *Come tomorrow! Monday. Come on. Tomorrow. Come on. Tomorrow!* I just want to see and spend time with her because I have missed her since she went back home two weeks ago. She is coming on Friday so I have to wait another whole week to see her. Darn, but oh well.

I went for a walk with my mom and it was beautiful out. It felt like spring! I could not believe it! We walked to Mrs. O's house to see if she was home. Nope. No luck. We walked for a mile and a half and I am surprise how well my mom did. I was proud of her!

My mom and I picked a date out for my Open House Party! I am excited about it! I have to go post it online. A couple of people have already invited me to their Open House this week so it was kind of a wake-up call for me. Mine is going to be on June 14th from noon until three o'clock. I picked the Sunday of the 21st, but my mom was worried about being too late and everybody would forget about it.

March 16, 2009

I worked some things out regarding how I am going to do my PowerPoint presentation with Mrs. Van, Mr. Hair, and Mrs. Doreen. So I feel a little bit better about it and I have to make touch-ups, but I think I am pretty much ready to go. I worked on it for three hours and by the end of fourth hour, I was sick of making it.

I had to answer some questions about my full-ride scholarship award from the University of Phoenix for the school's newspaper. They are going to, I guess, have the picture of me getting my scholarship, which Mr. Hair did a great job of capturing the moment! I am very pleased at that picture. Wow! Whooo weeeee! So I felt pretty cool that I am going to be in the newspaper because of my full-ride scholarship. I think that will help me "slap" some of the teachers and people's faces by saying, "Ha-ha! Look at me! I have a scholarship and I am disabled. I did it! Ha-ha!" Sometimes I wish that I could slap them in the face when they just see my disability and that is all they are willing to see in me. Why can't people get past and look past that to see the person who I really am? I think that would be easier for me in life, but I know that God made me exactly how He wants me. I just have to figure out what that purpose is still.

Mach 17, 2009

Mrs. Smiley met me this morning at school and helped me get off the bus. She congratulated me about my full-ride scholarship and gave me two hugs. She said, "So your mom is OK with you doing this?" "Oh yeah! Yep!" I said. "Well good! See your mom is a lot better with you leaving than she was with Ashley and Britney leaving," she said as she started walking backward to her bus. I have a confused look on my face then I thought: *Oh! She probably thinks that I'm going there and she doesn't realize I'm doing it online. Ha. I better e-mail her tonight to set her straight.* After school, Tammy asked if I was going to go there and I said that I wasn't and pretended like I was typing. She got what I meant, which I was glad about!

Mrs. Van and I timed my PowerPoint presentation. It has to be seven to ten minutes long and mine is 12 minutes, so I was very happy about that. Then we worked on a confusing story to read and follow for World Lit also.

Second hour, we had some time left to chitchat because we were finished with the questions that we had to do for the confusing story. Mrs. Van said, "I need new frames. I am going to get some that look just like yours. So next year we are going to look like twins!" "Yeah, but I won't be with you next year." I said. "Oh. Don't remind me of that." she said. I think she is still in denial about that, but oh well.

March 18, 2009

In the morning, I tried to find and hunt down Mrs. Doreen because she said that she was going to write down my battery number for the school's laptop that I use. It has been giving me issues by only staying charged for three hours instead of six hours and that is annoying. I need it to stay charged for six hours because I am in school for six hours. It just makes sense to me. Mrs. Doreen was not there and will not be in until next week so I thought: *Oh, OK. Why did you not tell me that in your e-mail to me?*

Second hour, Mrs. Van and I worked on the fun-confusing story in World Lit. I am kind of ahead of everybody so that feels good! Friday, I am going to have a vocabulary quiz that I am a little bit worried about, but of course, I have not been studying for! Tomorrow, in Child Development, I have a test and I have studied a little, but not like I should be studying.

March 19, 2009

I did not feel like waking up this morning so my alarm sounded the longest it has ever sounded in a long time. I just wanted to sleep and stay under my warm blankets!

I studied well for Child Development before supper, but after supper, I did not study at all. I turned on my iTunes, played around on the Internet, and uploaded my pictures of my second parents (Mr. and Mrs. Van), which I love a lot! Can you tell that I have a little "senioritis?" So I studied in first and fourth hours and I feel that I did well on the test. We will see shortly.

This weekend I will be gone! I am going to be at Alma with Ashley for Little Sibs Weekend! I am not going to be home until Sunday. So I will not be able to write until Sunday or Monday, so do not miss me too much OK? I have no idea what Ashley and I are doing this weekend. She called last Sunday and asked, "What do you want to do next weekend?" "I don't care. I will do whatever." I said.

Dimly Lit

"OK, we are going to sit in my room and stare at each other then." I yelled, "NOOOO!" "Then tell me what you want to do." Ashley demanded. I have to go pack soon.

Tomorrow I will get to see Aunt Nay Nay and spend time with her on the trip to Alma! So, yay!

March 22, 2009

I'm back! Did you miss me? OK. Here is what Ashley and I did on Little Sibs Weekend. Friday night, I ate food (which was OK), watched TV for a couple of hours, and then at eight o'clock, we watched this guy do mind reading things and psychology things. He was really good. After that we went to the grocery store and got snacks. Beer nuggets are good. Don't worry; it tastes like an elephant ear. Watched TV and slept in her cute house. Woke up and ate French toast sticks with Ashley's friends who are fun! Then Ashley had a Powder Puff game for a couple of hours. They won and then we ate supper, which was AMAZING! I had macaroni & cheese, a pretzel, two elephant ears, and ice cream that was set up like a fountain. Then we went back to the house and watched *House*. We went to their game room, and Ashley and I ate cotton candy, and had our picture taken in our Alma sport uniforms. We slid down a huge slide two times, went back to the house and watched *House*. Then we went bowling with her roommate, her roommate's friend, and Ashley's guy friend. The five of us hung out mostly all weekend. Bowled for a couple of hours and it was cool because they had glow lights going and other things that made it cool and fun! We bowled two games and then went home. Slept in and ate. Now I'm home again. I didn't go to bed until early morning both nights. It was so much fun!

March 23, 2009

Mrs. Van, Mrs. Doreen, and myself test-drive my PowerPoint presentation before World Lit. We ran it different ways and by 8:42 A.M. we had it down. So Mrs. Van and I went to World Lit with a cart full of equipment of technology stuff. I went first because Mrs. Van said that I would go first. I was a little bit mad when she that, but today, I was glad that I was first. I'm glad that I am over and done with it.

I was tired in the morning because of my fun weekend at Alma College! I was moody toward Mrs. Van when we were together, but after she was not with me in the afternoon, I was better. Poor Mrs. Van. She has been through a lot with me and then I treat her bad. I don't know how she does it to put up with me when I'm moody.

Mrs. Engel was so busy helping Chad with finishing up his exams, the Plan Test, and missed work today. I cannot figure out why he missed so much stuff, but I think it is because he was on vacation or he was sick.

Aunt Nay Nay is back here, at the house and I love it! She has brought back the excitement in our house, which I love and missed. She and my mom took down my things that were on the walls in my

Dimly Lit

room to get ready for my dad to paint. It looks weird and I felt weird in my room with bare walls.

Aunt Nay Nay will be my date for Prom, which I am really excited about! I have asked so many guys to be my date, but of course, they turned me down. I started asking back in January because that is how much I REALLY wanted to go. It's my senior and last Prom so I have to and WANT TO go!

March 24, 2009

My mom woke up to my alarm sounding off because she was sewing a dress until two o'clock in the morning. Aunt Nay Nay did not hear my alarm either, and supposedly, she was going to get me ready. I do not know who said that she needed to practice, but she is. She is going to get me ready in the morning because my mom is going to be in Chicago next Monday. I am laid back about the whole Aunt Nay Nay getting me ready thing. It is going to be like I have a sub, like I have when Mrs. Van can't work. No big deal.

Dimly Lit

Mrs. Engel changed her room around for me. That way it is easier for me to plug in what I need to plug in these days, which is a lot! It was kind of funny how she said it. She said something like, "Hey Em, go check out my room because I made it more handicapped accessibility so you don't turn me in." Laughs showered the room.

I told Mrs. Van about Aunt Nay Nay going to Prom with me and she reacted not how I thought she was going to. I was kind of disappointed, but oh well. Today she was sad about something. I could tell by the way she was acting. I mean, whom better (besides her family) can a person tell that, than her best friend! I mean, we have known each other for nine years! I think I know Mrs. Van quite well! Thank you very much! She told me why when we were in the bathroom. It was because Mrs. Kar is not going to have a job next year. They cried together and Mrs. Van going to find out about her job tomorrow night. I am REALLY HOPING that she has a job next year!

Dimly Lit

March 25, 2009

At school, Mrs. Van did her normal routine that she does in my first hour, which only takes her 10-minutes to do. But this morning it felt longer, and was longer, so I was worried. I started to think that she got caught up in talking to some people because that is normally what happens. If you knew her, you would understand completely what I am talking about! Then I thought that something bad happened to her, like she got hurt and the ambulance came for her. So, at 8:16 A.M., I set off to go look for her. Meanwhile, my heart is pulsating really fast because I am worried and scared. Down the elevator I go and stopped in Mrs. Doreen's office. I asked her, "Where is Mrs. Van?" "I don't know," she said. She helped me find her. Mrs. Van was upstairs. We must have missed each other while I was on the elevator. Mrs. Van and I talked about what she did. She thought that I was mad at her, but I was not at all. We did my World Lit homework, hugged, and read her book. Meanwhile, my blood pressure went back to normal.

Lunchtime was great because I laughed so hard at Mrs. Van that tears were dripping down my cheeks! At first, I was laughing a little for no good reason at all. Then I finished eating the Cheez-Its Twizzlers. I did not want anymore, but wanted Mrs. Van to wipe my mouth, so I pointed to the napkin to get that message across. She put the Twizzlers on the napkin and I started cracking up! How she put them on it and her facial expression was hilarious!

Just by the comments she made today, I could tell that she was worried about her meeting at 3:30 P.M. I felt hopeless because I want her to have a job next year, but I can't do anything for her to make that happen. I am frustrated also.

March 26, 2009

Aunt Nay Nay did everything this morning in terms of getting me fed, clothed, doing my hair (which I didn't like when I saw it at school after lunch, but oh well) and she also did my face. Twice

Dimly Lit

I had to tell my mom to go lie down and sleep, and that Aunt Nay Nay was doing a fine job. I knew that she did not get enough sleep. It was like I was being kind of a mom to my mom, which is funny to say. Aunt Nay Nay loves to talk (just like my mom does!) so she talked to Tammy in front of the bus for a long time! I kind of had the feeling that I would be late in getting to school, which was no big deal to me, this morning. I always beat Mrs. Van to school, so hey, why can't she beat me today?

    I saw from afar that Mrs. Van was heading toward me, and then she went back to the Resource room where we meet up in the morning. I thought with a smile: *Maybe she was going to look for me.* We got into "my office" and we did our normal morning routine. Of course, I was anxious to hear about her meeting last night after school. She doesn't have a job next year. My heart sank. Luckily, she told me before she left to do her runs so I had time to think while she was gone. I wanted to cry, but I did not. That is, at least, not until I got home. She came back and we started to do my World Lit homework. I glanced over at her to see if she was OK with the news and she said, "Don't give me that look." I looked at the wall right after she made that comment. I feel like I should be doing something, but I cannot.

March 27, 2009

This morning I had to tell my mom again to go back to bed because she went to sleep at 4:00 A.M. She only had an hour of sleep. My dad ate breakfast with me, and then he went back to bed when I was finished. I was hard on Aunt Nay Nay when she did my hair because I did not want to look and feel like I did yesterday. Even Mrs. Van liked it today. On the bus ride to school, the song ""Mayberry"" was on, so I was singing along and dancing because it is a good song.

I teased Mrs. Van about being gone to do her normal stuff. She said, "OK I will be back soon." "Yeah, like in a half hour." I said in a smart aleck tone. She smiled, laughed a little, and hit me on top of my head with the papers in her hand. I studied my vocabulary words for World Lit and she was back in 10-minutes. I was shocked and said, "Wow." She looked at the clock and smiled. We studied vocabulary and talked together.

In the bathroom, after my lunch, we hugged for the longest time, which I loved! We talked about the All-Nighters' Party and we used the restroom. Before she put me back into my wheelchair we hugged again. It makes me tickled pink when Mrs. Van says, "I love you" to me because she does not say it all that often.

It's the weekend. I did not want to go to school today because everybody, even Ashley, was home today. They were all gone when I came home from school, of course. So, I finished my homework so I can have fun this weekend! Yahoo baby!

March 29, 2009

Friday night, Uncle Mark came to our house right after work and he beat the rest of the gang. He teased Britney about her <u>little</u> car. It's not that little because I have ridden in it before. He and my dad talked for a little bit after dad changed out of his work clothes. Then the rest of the gang came home and we started to snack while the pizzas were cooking. Luke and Trevor were playing Hide-and-Go-Seek and air hockey while we were snacking. I showed my dad, Britney, Aunt Nay Nay, Mom, and Uncle Mark my story about my scholarship that was in the school's newspaper. Uncle Mark asked me questions about how it all works, which I thought was pretty cool. Then everybody ate supper and we popped in a movie. Trevor and Luke were not watching it, so we watched TV shows. I was tired and they left around 11:00 P.M. Aunt Nay Nay put me to bed and that was a joke because she can't lift me. Getting into bed is hard work!

On Saturday morning, I woke up at nine. My mom thought that I woke up early to say good-bye to her because she was leaving after work for Chicago. I said, "Yes," but that really was not the reason at all. After she left, and after breakfast,

Aunt Nay Nay helped me clean out the stuff that was under my bed and in my drawers. My dad was a "psycho-Nazi" about my drawers being cleaned. At first, I was mad at him for clearing my room out without me, and now the drawers. After we were done we watched *Fireproof*, which is my favorite movie. I love and so want the music to it. Then we went to church. After church, we ate at BBQ's. I was so hungry so I ate well! Then we went home and we watched *Jack & Jill*.

March 30, 2009

At 4:30 A.M. my dad was vacuuming which woke me up. I was mad, but thankfully, I fell back asleep. Aunt Nay Nay was ready and was waiting for my alarm to sound off. She came into my room like right away! I was surprised about how prompt she was, and said, "Wow!" I thought that I was going to have to knock on my wall to wake her up, but nope. Everything went fine and she did my hair right; even Mrs. Van liked it.

On the bus, the song ""Here Comes Goodbye"" played and that is my new favorite song. Of course, I danced and sang along to it because that is just who I am. I got to listen to the entire song too and it reminds me of graduation and saying "goodbye" to Mrs. Van. It was stuck in my head the entire day and I would sway from side-to-side. In the bathroom, Mrs. Van and I kind of slow danced a little bit. So that was kind of cool. In the morning before, I went to the bathroom I asked her to do me a favor and she said, "Yes." I said, "When you get home tonight, go on YouTube and look up that song." She said, "OK."

I found out that I (hopefully) will get my new battery after spring break, which makes me so happy because plugging it in to charge at school is annoying!

April 1, 2009

I had two tests today and the World Lit test was huge. I was a little bit nervous about that one, but I think I did OK. I studied like six hours for that test. During the test time, we had a lock down and Mrs. Van and I had to go into the library's back room to hide. We waited for a long time for an OK to go back working. I was by Mrs. D, Mr. Z, and Mrs. Van. It was cool because we small talked about kids, food they eat, and spring break. Of course, we talked about graduation and my college. Mr. Z reminded me that he wants to have lunch with me before I graduate.

I am kind of, and kind of not, surprised that nobody played an April fool's joke on me. I am not complaining at all.

It felt like Mrs. Van and I really talked today. It almost felt like old times, which I so want back because I REALLY miss it!

In Child Development we took our test, and then we got to hold and "play" with the fake babies. First, we watched the video on all about what to do and how the baby works. Then we got to hold the baby. Tomorrow they will cry and become alive. I was worried about missing the baby demo because I take longer to take tests so I wrote a note (with Mrs. Van's help) to tell her to come and get me when they started the demo. I ended up finishing without doing the essay before somebody came for me. I was proud of myself.

I had to finish my two essays from my tests at home because I type faster at home than I do on my laptop. Child Development's essay was not hard at all. World Lit was harder because I had to read four myths and answer some critical thinking questions.

April 3, 2009

Yesterday was an easy and boring day because I read *The Good Earth* for most of the day. I finished it, so today; I am working on the project on the first day of Spring Break. I am so excited that Spring Break is here! I walked with Mrs. Van and it felt like old times, sort of because we really talked. I don't know who said, "I love you" first, but when I heard that, my heart pulsated fast. I felt warm and fuzzy inside. I received two great hugs also. I think she and I said them a lot yesterday. Ah! I already missed her when I was watching TV last night with Aunt Nay Nay.

In Child Development the babies came alive and sometimes I felt like saying, "AH! Make them stop crying!" When you don't support the head, then they cry harder and longer! I hope I can take good care of it when it is my time. I signed up to take it home on May 12th and 13th.

When my dad came home from work, he was REALLY moody and not talkative. I thought at night: *I want to go back to school with Mrs. Van! I am much happier there than I am at home.* So Aunt Nay Nay and I stayed downstairs and watched a weird movie before supper. We saw a preview for it on another movie that we watched last weekend. The preview for it looked good, but the movie itself was weird. I didn't understand it at all.

April 6, 2009

We ate at a steakhouse on Friday night. Then we just went home and watched TV. We were planning on going to see the *Duplicity*, but Aunt Nay Nay did not feel good.

Saturday morning I woke up at nine o'clock, but I thought it was later than that so I hurried to see what time it was. My dad doesn't like me to sleep in until 11:30 A.M. so I kind of make myself wake up before that time. My mom and Aunt Nay Nay had a huge fight, so Saturday was kind of like walking on eggshells. While they were fighting upstairs, I worked on my World Lit book project, and I looked at pretty pamper orders with Britney. My tank tops that I ordered in February finally came. So I am going to be twins with Mrs. Van. We shopped for my prom dress and we found one. We shopped for my things. I am so excited about my prom dress. It's pink and white with ruffles on the bottom. We had to go and pick it up yesterday. My mom lucked out this year on not having to make my prom dress. I even said that to her too. After we shopped for my dress on Saturday, we saw the movie *Duplicity* and I didn't understand the movie at all. I asked my mom and Aunt Nay Nay if they understood it. Aunt Nay Nay said that she didn't, and my mom said that she did. I said, "Liar."

Sunday we got my prom dress and some other shirts too. We ate at lunch. I got a fake stick-on tattoo just to get Mrs. Van shook up because it's fun to do. Then we went to Aunt Amy's house and hung out with her and Uncle Mark for a few hours. We came home to eat supper with my dad and Britney. Then we watched TV.

April 9, 2009

Tuesday night was the first night I slept downstairs. Aunt Nay Nay is sleeping down there with me, which is nice. I had a hard time falling asleep Tuesday night, but last night I did not. I think it's because I went to bed at two in the morning. Tuesday night I thought about Alicia sleeping down there with me last June. Before Aunt Nay Nay and I slept, we watched *Ballet Shoes* with my mom and it was an OK movie. Aunt Nay Nay liked it.

Yesterday, Uncle Mark, Aunt Amy, Brooke, Trevor, Luke, and us looked at a building where my mom wants to start her own bridal business. It's huge and Aunt Nay Nay said that she could live upstairs and do her wax stuff that she is going to school for. I picked out a room that will be mine to do my online college courses. I picked it out because it has two windows in it. Everybody loved the building, but I think that it is not in a good location. We are talking about my mom having her own business many years down the road. After we finished looking at it, everybody came back to our house and we ate junk food, looked at magazines, and played whiffle ball (while the girls watched). I took many pictures with my Photo Booth camera of Brooke, Trevor, and Luke. Then we ate supper and watched *Yes, Man.* That is an OK movie. They left in a hurry to meet Brooke's "boyfriend." Then Aunt Nay Nay and I watched *Bedtime Stories* at 10:30 P.M. That is a good movie! We had to stay up late because my mom was sewing and she feels better when she knows people are awake with her.

Today Aunt Nay Nay and I are eating lunch with Mrs. O at Cheddar's. That was cool because Mrs. O and I reminisced a little bit. We talked about the present too, of course.

April 10, 2009

Last night I worked on my letter that I am writing to Mrs. Van. It's all about memories in our years that we have been together. I worked on it for two hours while my dad and Britney were sleeping, my mom was sewing, and while Aunt Nay Nay was doing make-up stuff online. I knew that we did not have a movie to watch so I worked on it because back in January (when I started it) I thought that I would have lots of time to work on it during Spring Break. That was before I knew that Aunt Nay Nay was going to live here too. I thought that there is nothing better to do than to work on writing her a letter because I thought that I would be bored on my

Spring Break. But, that didn't happen because of Aunt Nay Nay being here! I'm so happy about that!

My mom, Aunt Nay Nay, and I went to bed earlier than we have been going this week. It was 12:30, but I did not fall a sleep right away. When I looked at the clock last, it was 1:18. The reason that we went to bed "early" last night is because we had to drive Aunt Nay Nay to Kalamazoo for her appointment at church at eleven. I think Aunt Nay Nay set my alarm for 8:10. Boy, when it went off it scared me! I moaned too.

On the way there, we talked to Uncle Mark for most of the way. He talked about G, Trevor coming over tonight, and planning a 40th birthday party for Aunt Amy in May.

An hour later, Aunt Nay Nay was done with her meeting so, we drove her home. She is staying home for the weekend to have fun and hang out with her friends. When she got into the van I looked in her eyes to see if she cried. It didn't look like it.

April 11, 2009

Last night Trevor was over and he talked to my mom while she sewed banners for church. I guess he played around on the Internet too and watched TV. At first, my mom and dad were planning on hanging the banners up at church last night, but that never happened because my mom didn't finish them until midnight. My mom did that to herself because she talked to Dad and Trevor in the living room for a long time, and also at the supper table when Trevor was done eating and was just eating ice cream with me. She could have sewed during that time, but nope. So, my mom said that Trevor and I had to wake up early this morning to go hang them up. He and I did not have to wake up early, so that was cool.

Trevor did not sleep with me downstairs like I thought he was going to do. That was the first time I slept downstairs by myself since my room is getting painted. I had a little harder time falling asleep, but oh well.

My dad made us waffles for breakfast. Then I worked on Lesson 15 for my BYU College writing class. Trevor talked to my dad non-stop and I think my dad did not want him to. So he gave Trevor a job to do, which was putting a chip down, waiting 15-minutes and sucking up the ants. Trevor liked doing that I could tell. Then I watched a half-hour war movie with him. That was my break from working on the lesson.

April 13, 2009

Easter morning, we ate Tammy's French toast casserole and it is amazing! Then we went to church and came back and ate our Easter dinner at two o'clock in the afternoon with Britney. The Easter bunny brought me a chocolate bunny and Reese's Pieces. Everybody (but mostly Britney) ate them all. Aunt Connie, Oompa, Aunt Nay Nay, and Ashley called. It was cool that they called. All day I worked on Lesson 15 while my mom and dad worked on my room. They didn't get done with it until ten o'clock.

Dimly Lit

I did not sleep well at all in my new pink room. I only got two hours of sleep. I could not sleep because I was excited. I thought that today I would be tired, but I was not at all. So I was glad about that.

Mrs. Van is tan from going to Myrtle Beach. She talked to me a lot when I was walking during first hour, which was nice.

I slept for two hours and I was fine today.

April 26, 2009

Well, Prom was awesome! Aunt Nay Nay and I got ready for the Prom pretty much the entire day. Man, it's hard work being a girl! We took some pictures at home with my parents and the two of us. For supper we had Cheddar's and ate it in the van. Then we went to the bridge to take pictures with my group of friends, but nobody was there because it was raining. They are chickens. We still took a couple of pictures when it was raining. Off to Prom! We arrived there a few minutes early and Mrs. Jumpy told me how to get everywhere by using the elevator quickly. I was confused, but Aunt Nay Nay and I figured it out. Then we took pictures and danced the night away! It was nice to have Aunt Nay Nay along because she was my photographer when I wanted pictures with my friends. And I got to be myself when I danced so I think that was what it made it so much fun. I danced with three friends. There was a photo booth so Aunt Nay Nay and I did that toward the end of the night. When we left the Prom, everybody received a T-shirt and a bag. We didn't go to bed until one o'clock in the morning.

May 29, 2009

Graduation day had finally arrived! May 28, 2009 baby! I woke up at 6:45 A.M. at the sound of my alarm. I didn't hit it to stop it from sounding because I wasn't in the mood. My mom came in my room really fast and we got ready. Mrs. Van arrived at my house 10-minutes early so my mom was hurrying to get me finish getting ready. I said, "Calm down. Don't hurry." Of course, she didn't listen to me! Mrs. Van and I set off to go to the

Dimly Lit

Hayworth Center at Hope College. Mrs. Van and I found it easily. When she was operating my lift, she put it down on the ground before I was on it. That became the joke of the day between us! At breakfast, Aleasha offered to feed me and I said that she could. I felt bad because it was Mrs. Van's and my last day together before I graduate. But it was OK. I ate eggs that were weird tasting, an apple tart, two pieces of French toast, and two glasses of milk. While we were eating, they played our senior video, and I couldn't see it very well from where I was sitting. I ordered one so I can watch it at home after I get it. Then Mr. Runner and Mr. Black told funny jokes about the people they know really well. Most of them were funny and everybody cracked up laughing, but some of the jokes were mean. After they were done, Mrs. Jumpy and the Class Council put on the raffle. Some of the prizes were sweet.

Everybody walked to the De Vos Field house to practice for graduation. Before it started, we had to take some pictures as a whole class. After that, they gave us the rundown for graduation. Then we received our alumni T-shirts. After everybody left, Mrs. Jumpy and Mr. Fern wanted me to practice riding on stage. I did that twice. I took a couple pictures with my closest friends. Mrs. Van and I sat in the van opening gifts that I got for her. She loved them. Then I was hungry so we ate at Happy Place. I ate a cheeseburger and a chocolate shake. She had fries and a diet coke. She bought a cheeseburger for Mr. Van. We ate lunch with Erica and that was nice. Mrs. Van and I drove to my house and arrived there about 1:30. Mrs. Van talked to my mom and told her the scoop about graduation. They wanted me to take a nap and I kind of wanted to, but I didn't. What a surprise, right? I fooled around on the Internet instead.

    I started getting ready around 3:00. My mom, Dad, and I arrived at De Vos on time when I had to be there, which was an hour earlier than when the graduation ceremony started. Everybody thought it was lame to arrive that early. While we

Dimly Lit

were waiting, everybody, it seemed like, was taking pictures. When we were about to walk out, my nerves were getting stronger by the minute. Everything went smoothly. Afterwards I took many pictures, received a lot of hugs, and I said, "Thank you" of bunch of times.

Then my mom, Dad, and I arrived home when Ashley and Britney were arriving home. We took some pictures of all of us by my balloons that Ashley and Britney bought me. I had to hurry up and change into my comfy clothes for the All-Nighter. Then I had a few minutes to eat something before Mrs. Van arrived. When she arrived, I gave her a hug. We went to school and waited to go somewhere for supper, which was a surprise. The seven buses left at 10:30 P.M. Mrs. Van knew where we were going, of course, but I said to follow the buses. She said that the buses took us for a long ride. We went to Sunnybrook Country Club. I ate two different kinds of pasta dishes, cheese sticks, and water. Everybody was asking Mrs. Van where we were going next. I laughed, smiled, and felt bad for her, but she handled it just fine. Then we went to the second surprise spot, which ending up being the high school. It was decorated like a cruise ship. It was really cool! A caricaturist drew my face and I love my picture! Mrs. Van and I dressed up in swimming stuff and had our picture taken. I ate ice cream, candy, two slices of pizza, a bread stick, and drank a Coke! We watched people get tattoos, DJ contests, a volleyball game, mini-games that gave out prizes, jumpy things, basketball, water polo, swimming, belly flop contests (those were funny to watch), diving for cash, casino, and an AWESOME hypnotist. It was SO funny!

Around 2:30 A.M. we began to get REALLY tired! I'm can see why Coke is VERY important now! I was so thankful for it at that time! Around 5:30 A.M. we got our door prizes and raffle prizes and it was time to go home and SLEEP! I was surprise how well Mrs. Van stayed up! We told my mom and Dad bits and pieces of the night/morning. Mrs. Van and I said goodbye and hugged for one last time. My mom and I waved to Mrs. Van as she was driving away in the light of the morning sky. I showed my mom my prizes and cartoon of my face. I said goodbye to my dad as he was leaving for work. I fell in bed and didn't wake up until 1:30 P.M. I am a GRADUATE FROM HIGH SCHOOL! YAHOO!

Knowing that Mrs. Van was going to hang out with me next year while my parents and sisters are gone, helped saying "good-bye" to her so much easier. All year I was trying to keep Mrs. Van at arm's length (didn't work so well) to make this "good-bye" easier for us, but I didn't have to. My mom told me this news back in February. I didn't know how to react. I was happy about it, but confused

June 1, 2009

I am in the Advance newspaper. Here's a copy of the story. "Scholarship rewards attitude and overcoming obstacles" by Cathy. Hudsonville High

School graduate Emily Zondlak was chosen as the recipient of a University of Phoenix full-tuition scholarship, awarded through a Michigan Teacher of the Year.

Zondlak received the scholarship from Jennifer, a teacher at Hudsonville's Baldwin Street Middle School. Jennifer was named Michigan Teacher of the Year in fall 2008, and has represented teachers at a number of statewide functions.

"I chose Emily because of the challenges she has overcome," Jennifer wrote. "She exemplifies what it means to be a Phoenix." Jennifer sought information from high school teachers in her search for the scholarship recipient. "Emily is such a testimony to overcoming obstacles, setting high grade and reaching them, and remaining positive in the face of adversity."

Zondlak, who has cerebral palsy, uses a wheelchair and said she has had to work harder on academics than most students. She communicates

Dimly Lit

by e-mail and a speech recognition computer. University of Phoenix offers its programs online.

Zondlak has been assisted in her high school years by special-education teacher Engel. "The scholarship," Engel said, "provides Emily the opportunity for post secondary learning where she will be evaluated on her abilities."

"In high school, she enters the classroom and everyone sees her disability. In the Phoenix program, many of the courses are online. It levels the playing field. She will be accepted for what she can do."

"I feel excited and very happy to have received such an honor," Zondlak wrote. She will major in English, and hopes to write books about her experiences living with a handicap. "This scholarship will help me achieve my career goals by allowing me to further my education and gain the knowledge needed to become an author."

Jennifer said, " Getting acquainted with Zondlak has given me the chance to see that all students can succeed, especially when their teachers, families, schools, communities, and peers rally behind them."

June 24, 2009

I am in the Advance newspaper again! "Hudsonville grad receives Johnson scholarship award." "Emily Zondlak, a 2009 graduate of Hudsonville High School, is the recipient of this year's David Johnson Memorial Scholarship, awarded by Doug and Margo." The scholarship is named for their son, who died July 19, 1989, shortly before his 16th birthday of a malignant brain tumor. Had he lived, he would have graduated from Hudsonville High School in 1992.

The scholarship was established by Doug and Margo to honor and reward other students who "struggle with adversity, demonstrate courage, and inspire caring," Margo wrote. "We think those are qualities that David demonstrated."

Zondlak, who has cerebral palsy, uses a wheelchair and communicates via computer. She will be a student in an online program from Phoenix University. She plans to major in English, with a career emphasis in writing. The Johnson scholarship will be used to help cover college-related expenses.

Zondlak also was the recipient of a scholarship for tuition from Phoenix awarded through teacher, Jennifer, Michigan's 2009 Teacher of the Year.

My College Experience

September 12, 2009

This is how it's like going to University of Phoenix online. I check in every day and see if there's anything new. If not, I see if anyone left me messages, or I will ask questions. This is called 'threaded discussion,' a series of connected messages posted to a forum; as with e-mail, topical messages are read and replied to, and conversations can take place in a "threaded" manner. This is located in the forum, which is a component of an online classroom in, which threaded discussions take place; some forums are public to all, and others are privately used by specific students and instructors. Then I do my homework. It's kind of like e-mailing, but you have homework and stuff to do. I receive what is called feedback, which means my instructor will provide grades and comments on my assignments. He or she will send to something that no other classmates will see, but just the two of us can see and communicate. My instructors, classmates, and I can be online at the same time, but it rarely happens. We all can access the materials at anytime. Communication between my instructor and classmates who are not together at the same time is called 'asynchronous communication.' Examples of this could include e-mail, fax, threaded discussions, postal mail, etc.

December 6, 2009

Last week Tuesday, Mrs. Van and I surprised Alicia by stopping by her house since I knew Alicia had MOVED BACK! She called me on Black Friday and we talked for a long time. Talking on the phone was hard because of my speech. Anyways, Tuesday Mrs. Van and I were going to hang out with Erinn for our monthly get together. I knew Alicia was back so I asked Mrs. Van if we could bring Alicia along. She said, "Yes!" So, we had to come up with a plan to tell Alicia. Mrs. Van wasn't suppose to know about Alicia moving back because Alicia wanted to surprise Mrs. Van. I blew that secret out of the water! Alicia still doesn't know that I told Mrs. Van! So Mrs. Van and I drove over to Alicia's house. Her dad was outside. Mrs. Van and he talked for a while. Finally, he got Alicia and we hugged hard and for a long time! It felt GREAT!

Alicia came with us to Erinn's! We talked, ate snacks, took pictures, and watched the *Elf* movie. I was so happy that day because I was hanging out with my three best friends ALL at the SAME TIME!

This Friday, my mom, Alicia, and I are going Christmas shopping together. My dad has kicked my mom and I out of the house because he is having a Christmas party for work. I just need to buy two gifts. Maybe we will see a movie also.

June 5, 2010

Last month, I went to the *Revue Show* at the high school with Mr. and Mrs. Van, Alicia, and Erinn. The *Revue Show* is a show where the students sing songs that everybody knows, or should know. They act, sing, and dance. Halfway through the show, the students take a break and the audience can take a bathroom break or talk to friends.

While halftime was going on, high school students in the audience were running around and being loud. I thought: *Man! I am sure glad I am not in high school anymore. Was I that immature like that?* I saw a couple people who I knew and I talked to them. That was so cool. Afterwards Mrs. Van invited Alicia, Erinn, and I to have a sleepover at her house. Mr. Van didn't want to come along with us girls to the grocery store so he got dropped off at the house and we went to Happy Place for shakes. Then we went to the grocery store because Alicia and Erinn wanted to get their moms something for Mother's Day.

We went to Mrs. Van's house and Mr. Van asked what took us so long. I told him what we did and he was waiting for us to have supper. I felt bad for making him wait to eat. He ended up eating supper alone. Mrs. Van took pictures of Alicia, Erinn, and I. Then all us of watched *Shrek the Third*. It has adult humor, which I understood, and which I was proud of myself for. Then we got ready for bed and we three girls slept downstairs in their basement.

Mr. and Mrs. Van had a heater running, but we were still cold. We watched another movie, looked at Alicia's pictures that she wanted me to see, talked, and played games. We went to bed at 4:00 A.M. and woke up at 9:00 A.M. We had breakfast and Mrs. Van watched *Mr. Mom* with us. I feel SO BLESSED to have four friends who love me and treat me like a person and not a disabled person! I had some moments with each of my four friends that I will cherish forever! Moments that made me love my four friends more and which grew our friendship!

Last month on a Wednesday night, Mrs. Van invited my mom and I to her church to hear a speaker speak about friendship. It made me think about a few different friends. The speaker invited some people to talk about a certain thing that was special about their friends. Mrs. Van spoke about me and how I am kind through my words. When she stood and was walking toward the front, I thought: *Oh please no. Don't talk about me.* You really don't know how much a friend loves and appreciates you until he or she says or writes something about you. Afterwards I found out Mrs. Van's sister-in-law cried while Mrs. Van was talking about me. I am a friend with her sister-in-law so I was like, "Aw!"

Alicia, what she calls "moved out" (I call it ran away), of her house. Alicia couldn't handle her adopted mom anymore. Alicia is living with her grandparents and her real dad. It was a drama filled world for a few weeks last month. I'm going to see her on the 26th, which I don't know how I should feel.

August 2, 2010

After church, my mom and I went to an event called The 99 by Studio 27 and it was awesome! We went through several rooms in a huge tent. Adults and kids reenacted skits of a drunk-driving accident, a drug house, beatings, a girl who shot herself because she gave up on life, what Hell is like, what Jesus had to go through for us, and had people who prayed for you. It was scary, but a good wake-up call. Drugs, alcohol, and violence kill every day 99 people.

Did I tell you that I'm taking horseback riding lessons this summer? It started in June and went every other week. My horse's name is Molly and she is brown. I have to brush her first thing when Mrs. Van and I arrive to Al's. Then I ride Molly in a corral with a girl riding with Molly and me.

The first time I rode Molly, I had a death grip on the horn of the saddle. My second lesson I did much better and didn't grab the horn at all. Al, my teacher, is very impressed about how awesome I am doing. We crack jokes between each other during my lesson. It is fun! Al asked me to be in a horse show at the Hudsonville Fair Grounds after my second lesson. The reason why he wants me to be in a few shows is to be an inspiration for others. Al wanted me to do a show in Grand Rapids, but Mrs. Van said, "Let's go small first, and then go big if Em wants." On the 10th at 7:00 P.M. at Hudsonville Fair Grounds, I'll be in a horse show! My mom has a week to sew a special horse shirt, which means late nights for her. I have to wear the shirt, jeans, boots, a cowgirl hat, and a big belt. I have to make Molly walk, trot, stand still in one spot, and turn the correct way.

August 17, 2010

     I had my first horse show Tuesday the 10th. I placed FIRST! I arrived at the fairgrounds at 7:00 P.M. and watched other riders compete in shows. That was good for me to see what I needed to improve on before my show. I visited with friends and family members. At some points, I got nervous, but I think that's normal. I think about 8:30 P.M. I practiced with Abby on Molly. We visited my friends and family members on Molly while being photographed. Then I said a prayer to God and we started the show.

The judge said I couldn't compete while I was walking Molly in the corral. Abby said that we cleared it. The judge said, "Oh, OK." The reason why the judge said that was because Abby rides behind me to make sure I don't fall off! Once we were down a little ways away from the judge, Abby said, "We will show her!" We laughed. We walked for a while then trotted, reversed Molly, and did the same thing. After that, we stood in the middle and waited to see who placed. Molly did very well!

When they called the first place winner, I heard Emily something. I thought: *OK, it's not me. That's cool.* But Abby patted me on my shoulder and said, "Em, it's you!" I started tearing up as I was riding to get my ribbon. Many people congratulated

Dimly Lit

me and took pictures of Molly, Abby, Al, and I. Friends are commenting on my pictures, which is neat! I felt SO BLESSED to have many friends and family members to support me!

About The Author

At the age of eight, Emily developed a desire to become an author to communicate with people. Many people have the impression that Emily is not smart because of her disability. Before Emily decided to declare Jesus Christ as her personal Lord and Savior of her life, Emily wanted to prove people wrong and complete chapters in life that they do not think it would be possible, such as graduating with a diploma from high school and earning degrees in college.

God blessed Emily by making her dream of being an author become a reality! Emily had to be willing to be molded into Jesus Christ's image before His plan and her desire came to completion! After being turned down by seven publishing companies, God blessed Emily with an open door of possibilities for being a published author!

God has chosen Emily to write books. He's fulfilling her dream and desire to impact His kingdom! Seventeen years later, God has made Emily an author! Proverbs 16:9 states, "We can make our plans, but the Lord determines our steps." With God's Holy Spirit's help, Emily has published Open H†S Word and Chap†er By Chap†er also!

www.ingramcontent.com/pod-product-compliance
Lightning Source LLC
Chambersburg PA
CBHW052145110526
44591CB00012B/1862